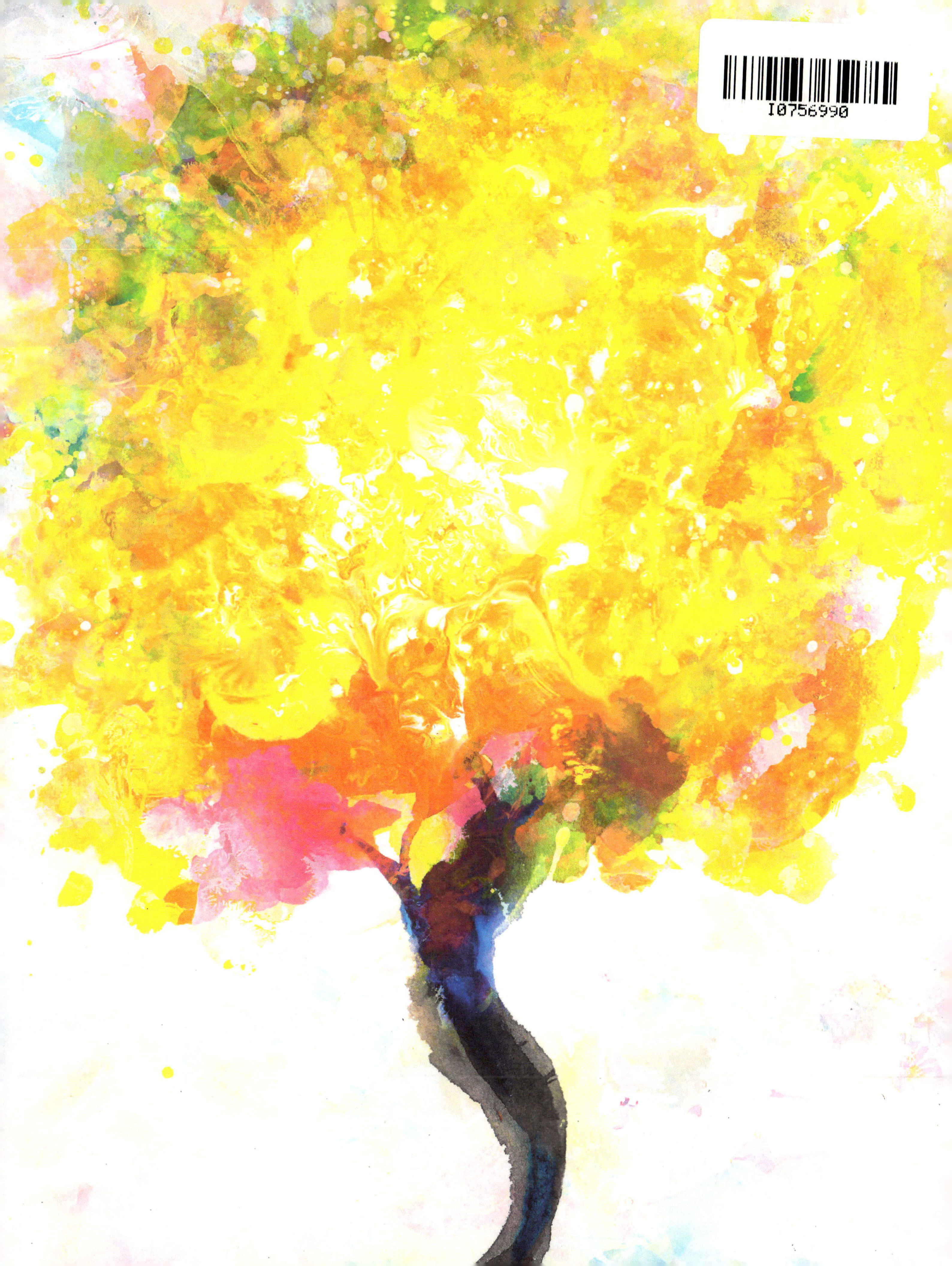
I0756990

RINGO THE GINKGO

Written and illustrated by
Arshak Martirosyan

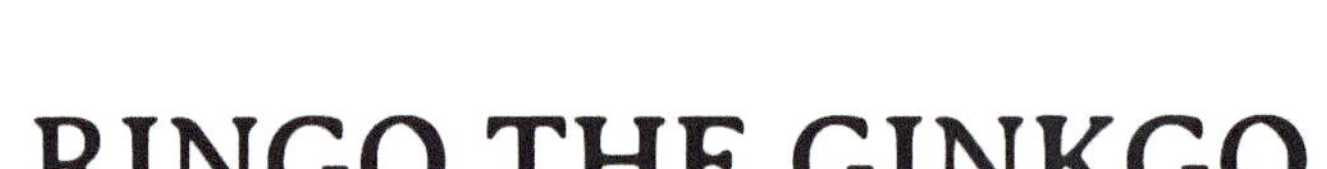

https://www.instagram.com/ringotheginkgo/
https://www.amazon.com/dp/B0CVNHJ8FL

ISBN 979-8-218-29461-8

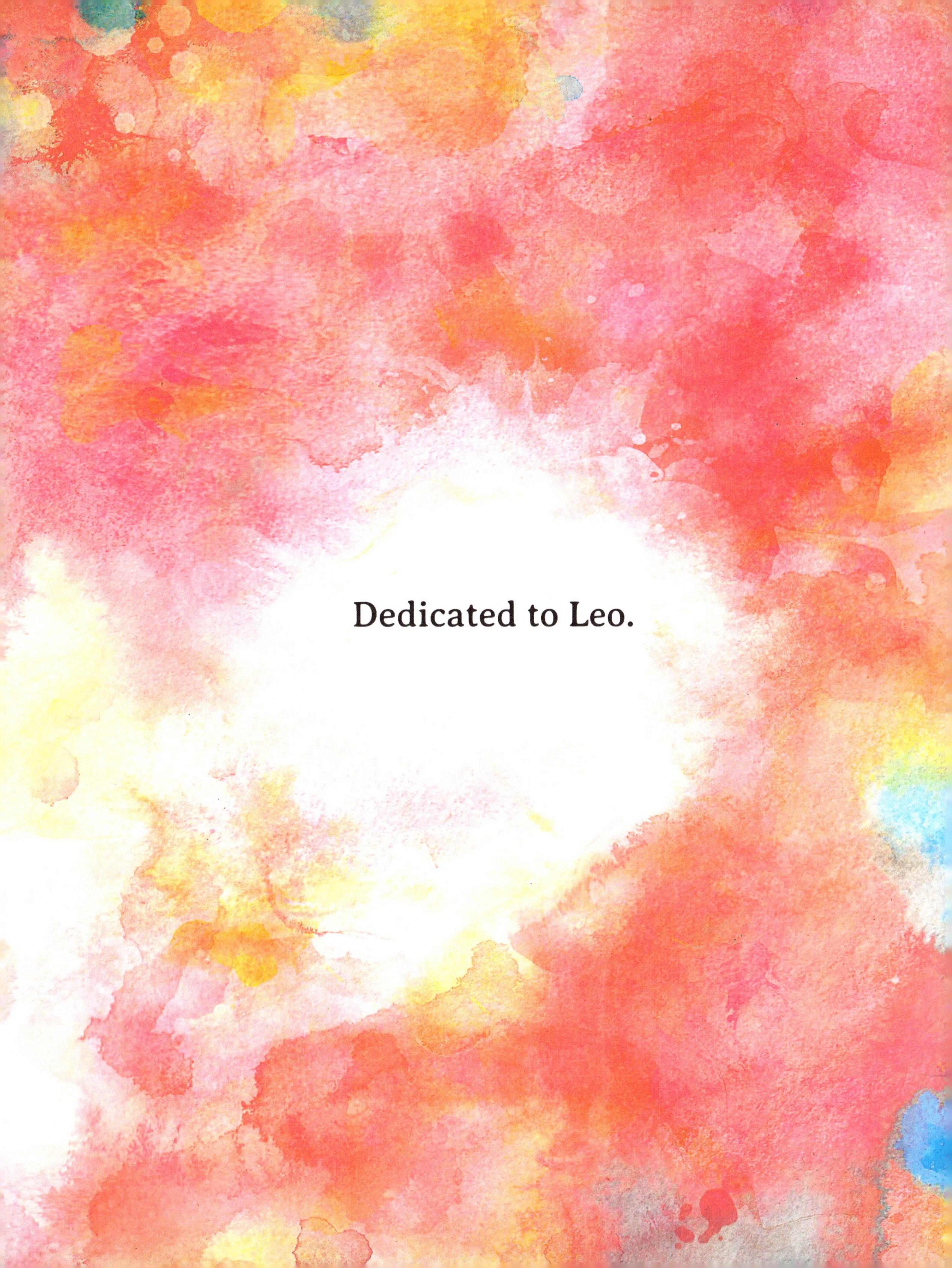
Dedicated to Leo.

This

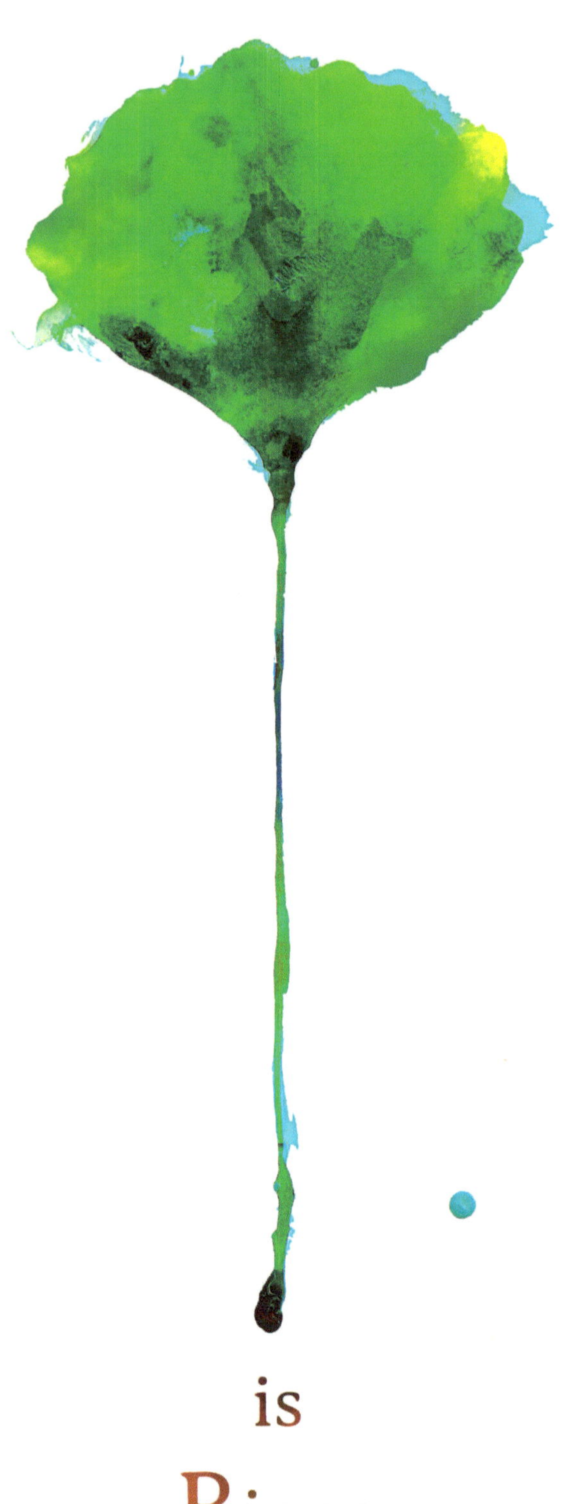

is

Ringo

Ringo is a ginkgo leaf.

Ginkgos
are beautiful
trees...

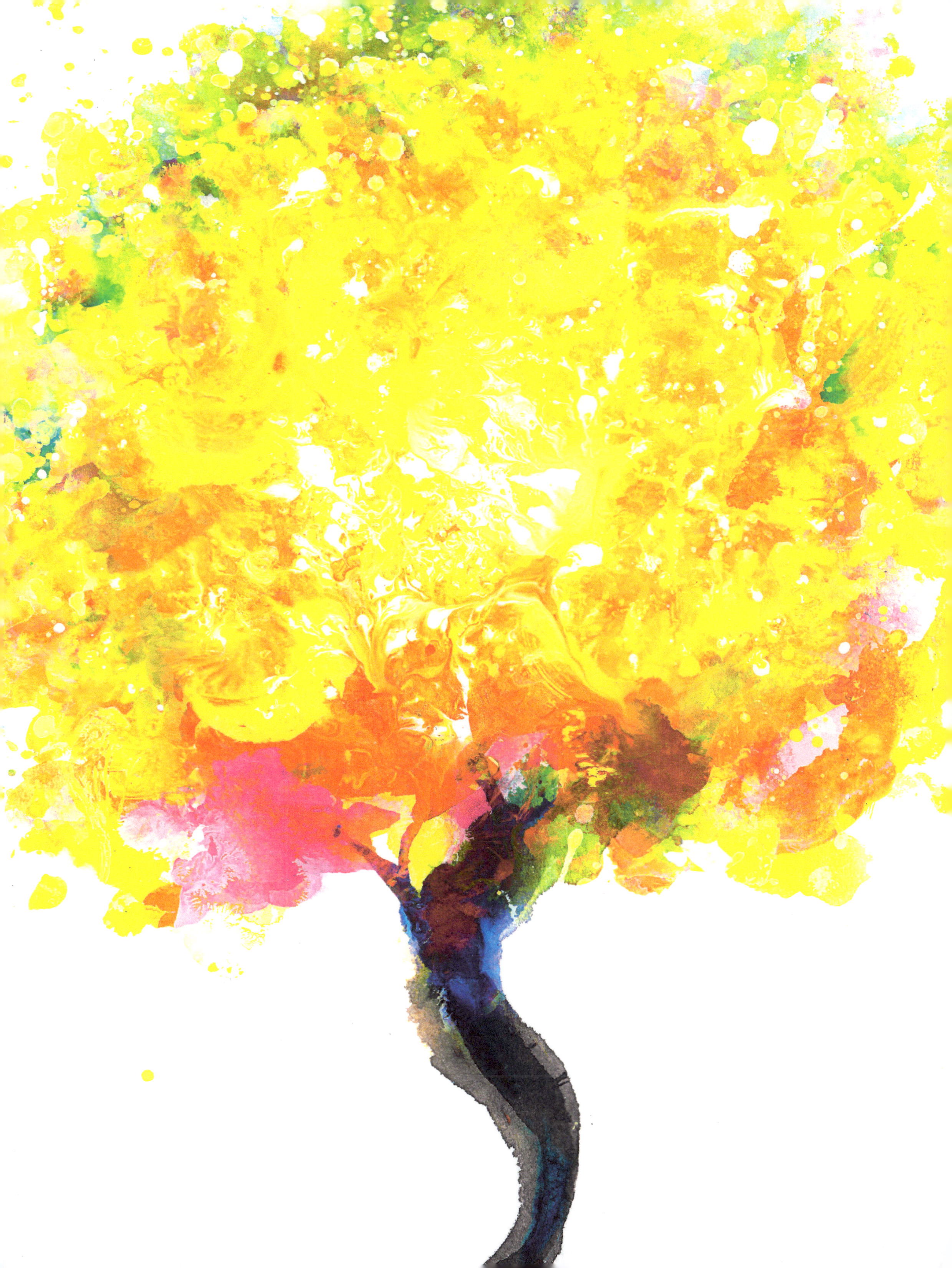

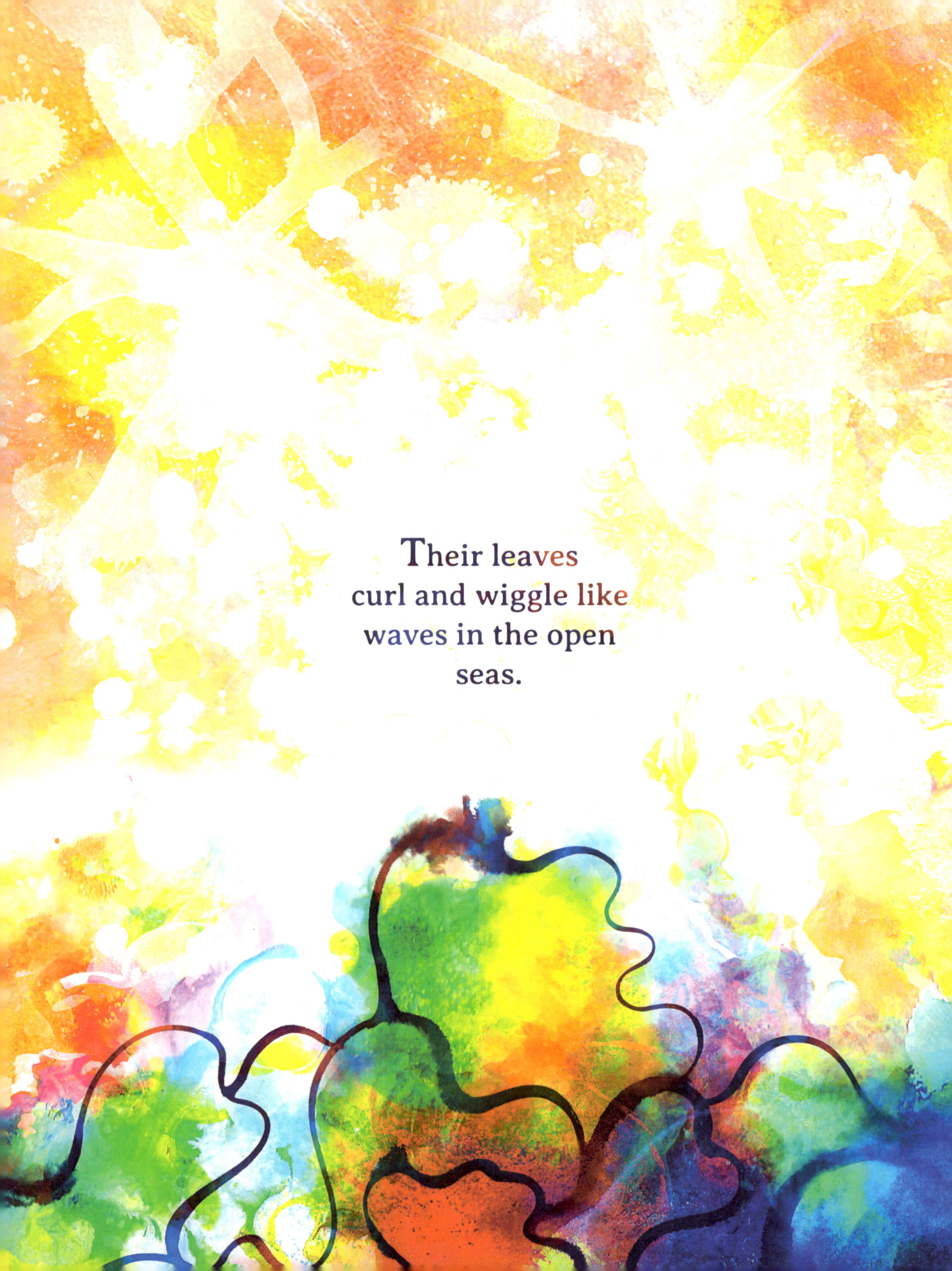

Their leaves
curl and wiggle like
waves in the open
seas.

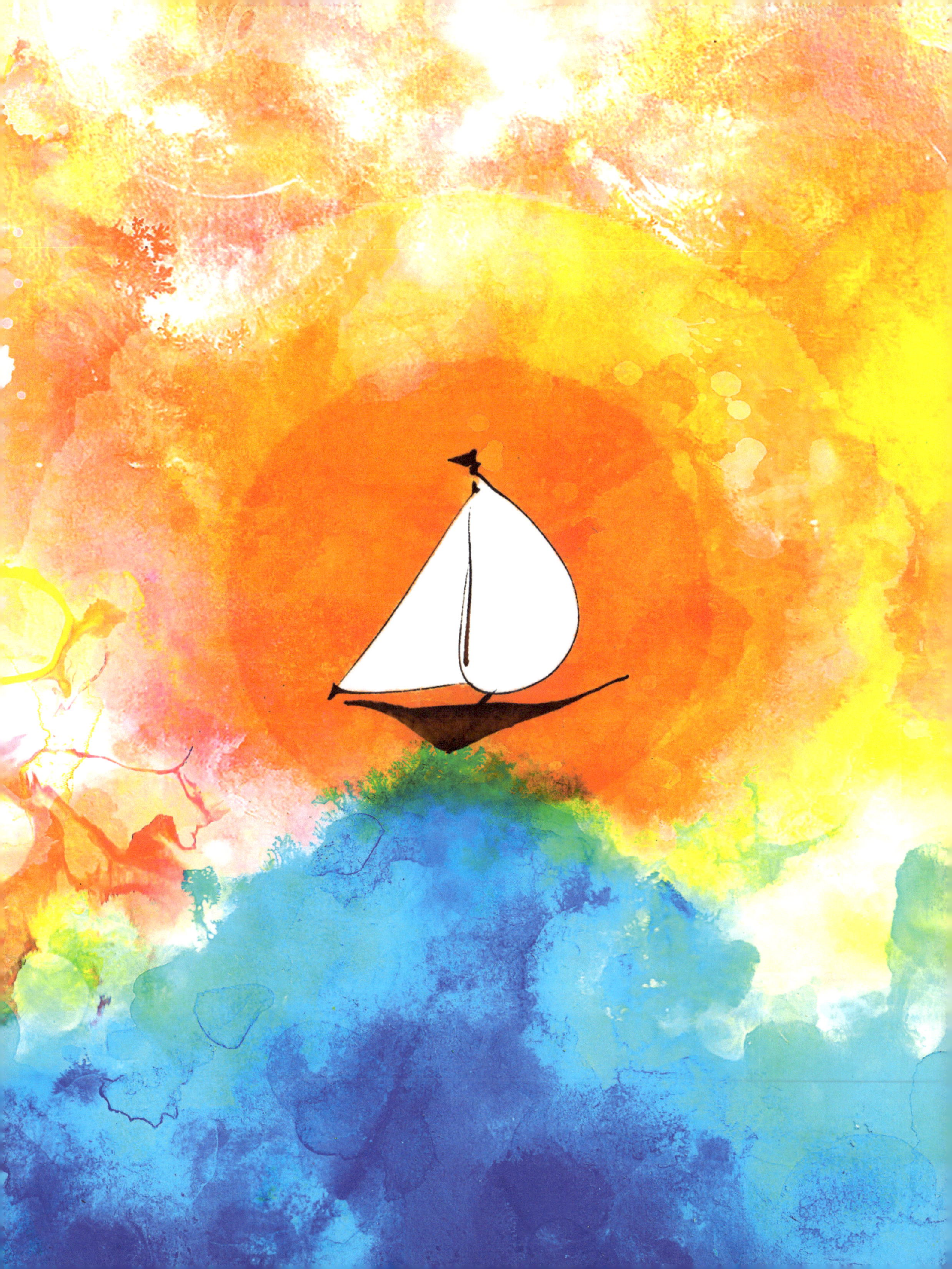

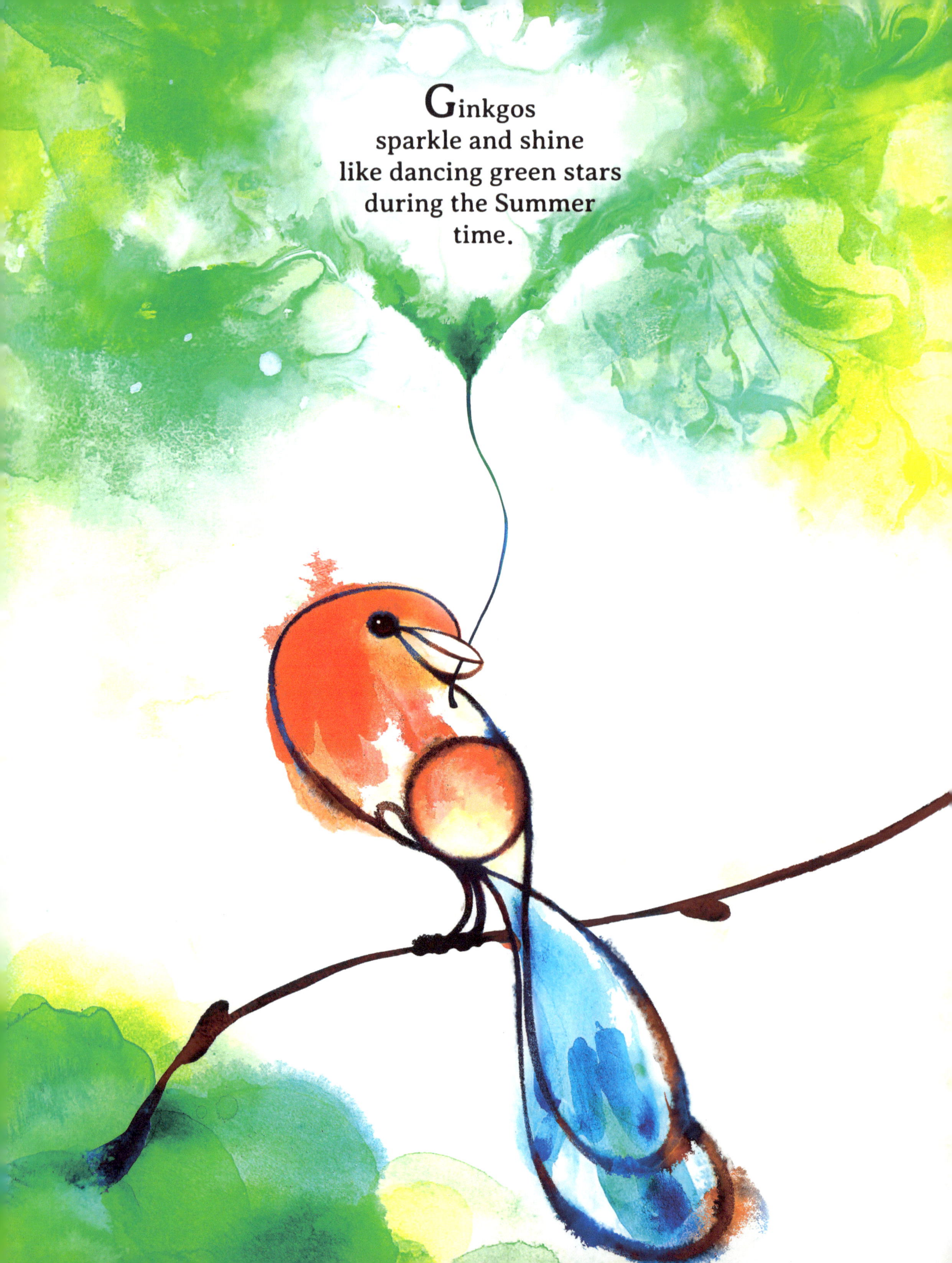

Ginkgos
sparkle and shine
like dancing green stars
during the Summer
time.

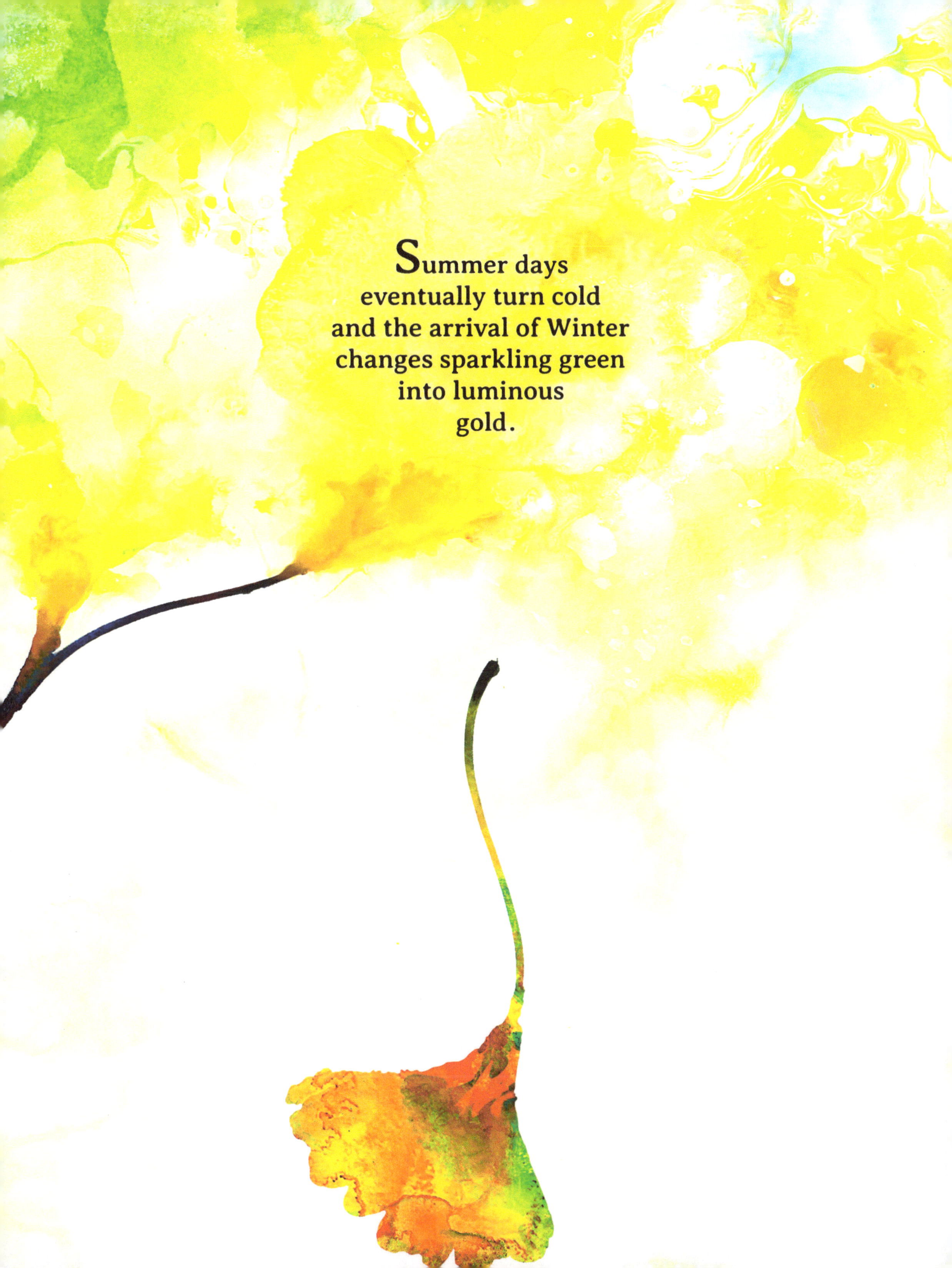

Summer days
eventually turn cold
and the arrival of Winter
changes sparkling green
into luminous
gold.

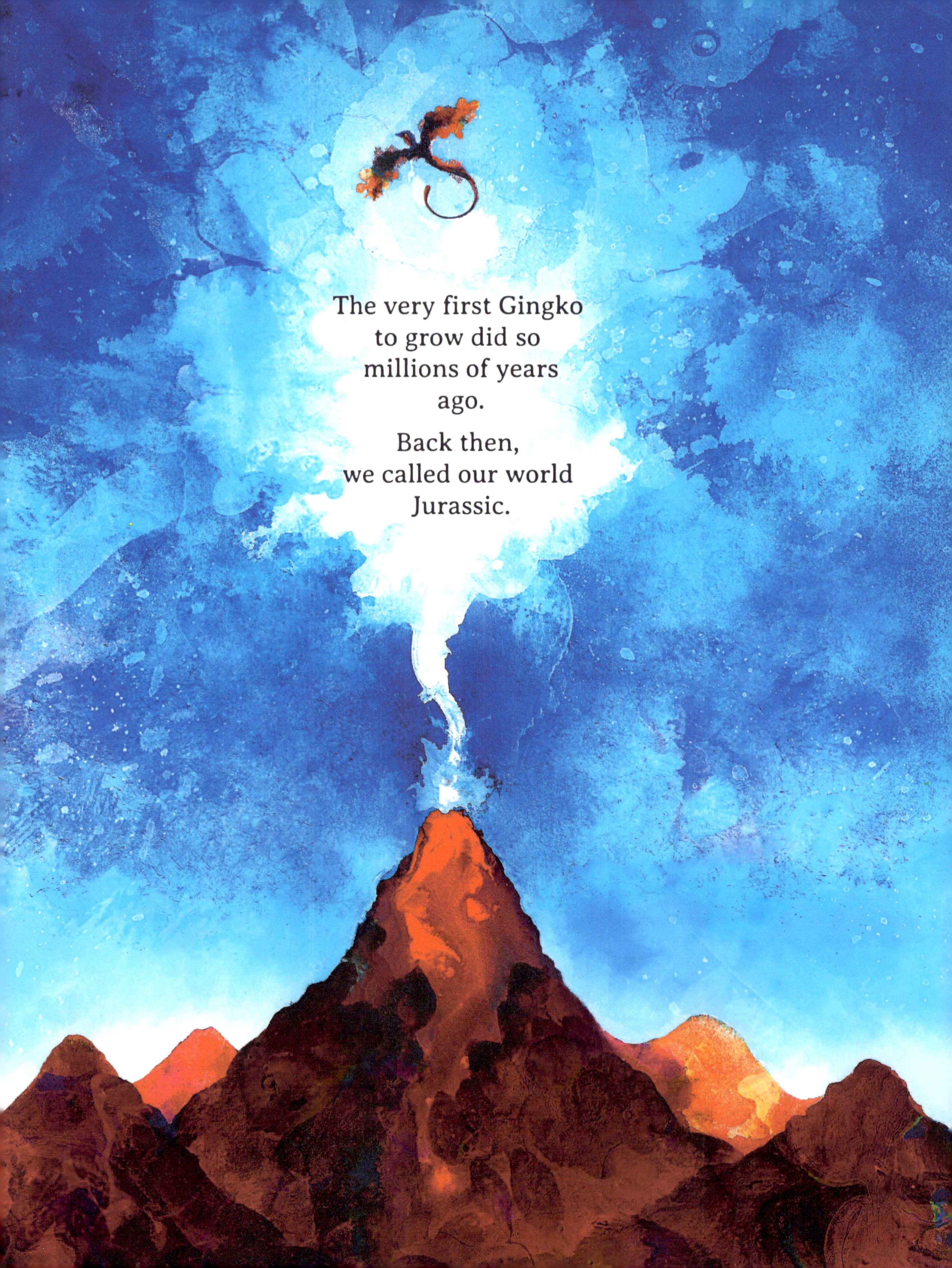

The very first Gingko
to grow did so
millions of years
ago.

Back then,
we called our world
Jurassic.

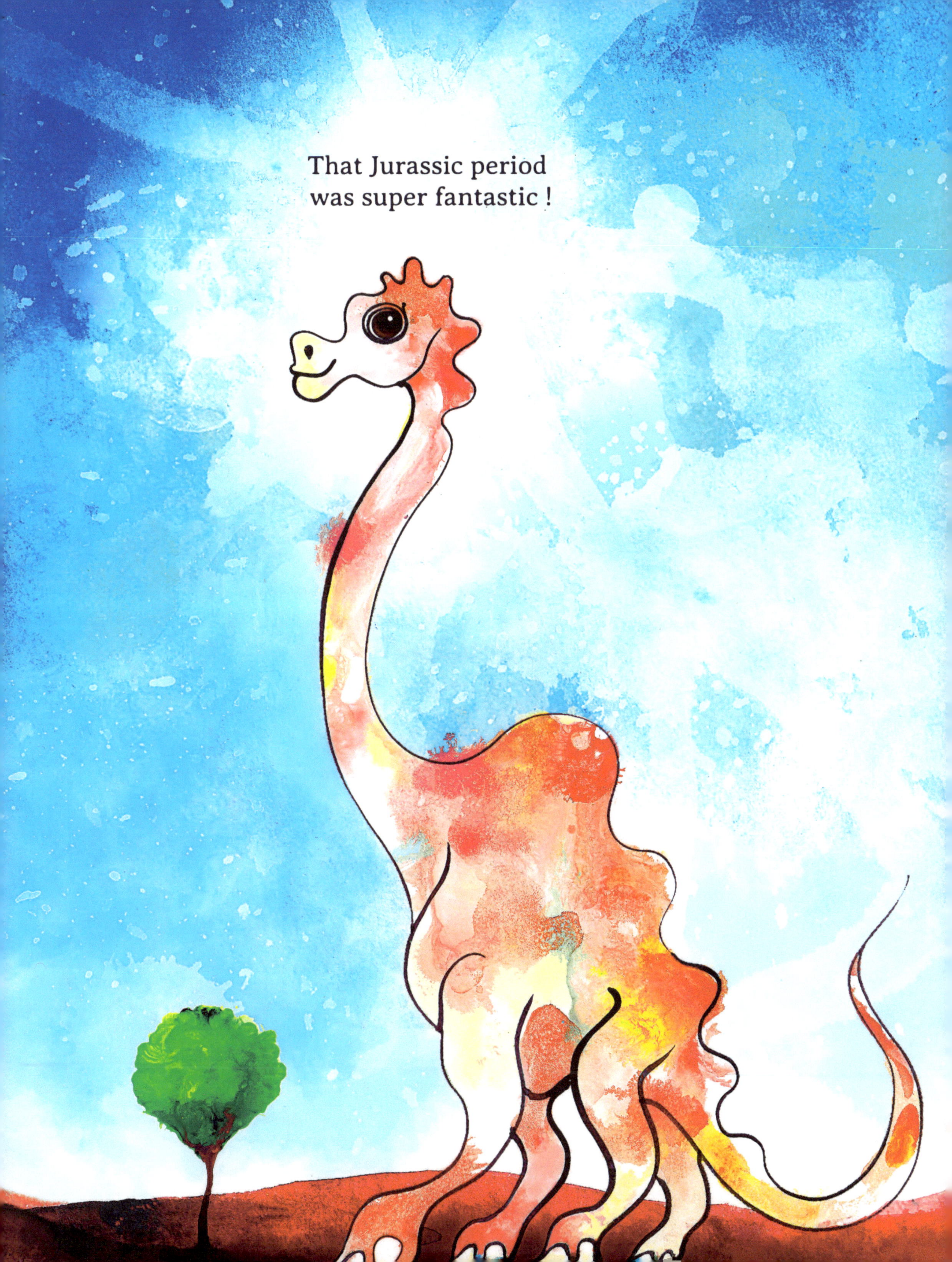

That Jurassic period
was super fantastic !

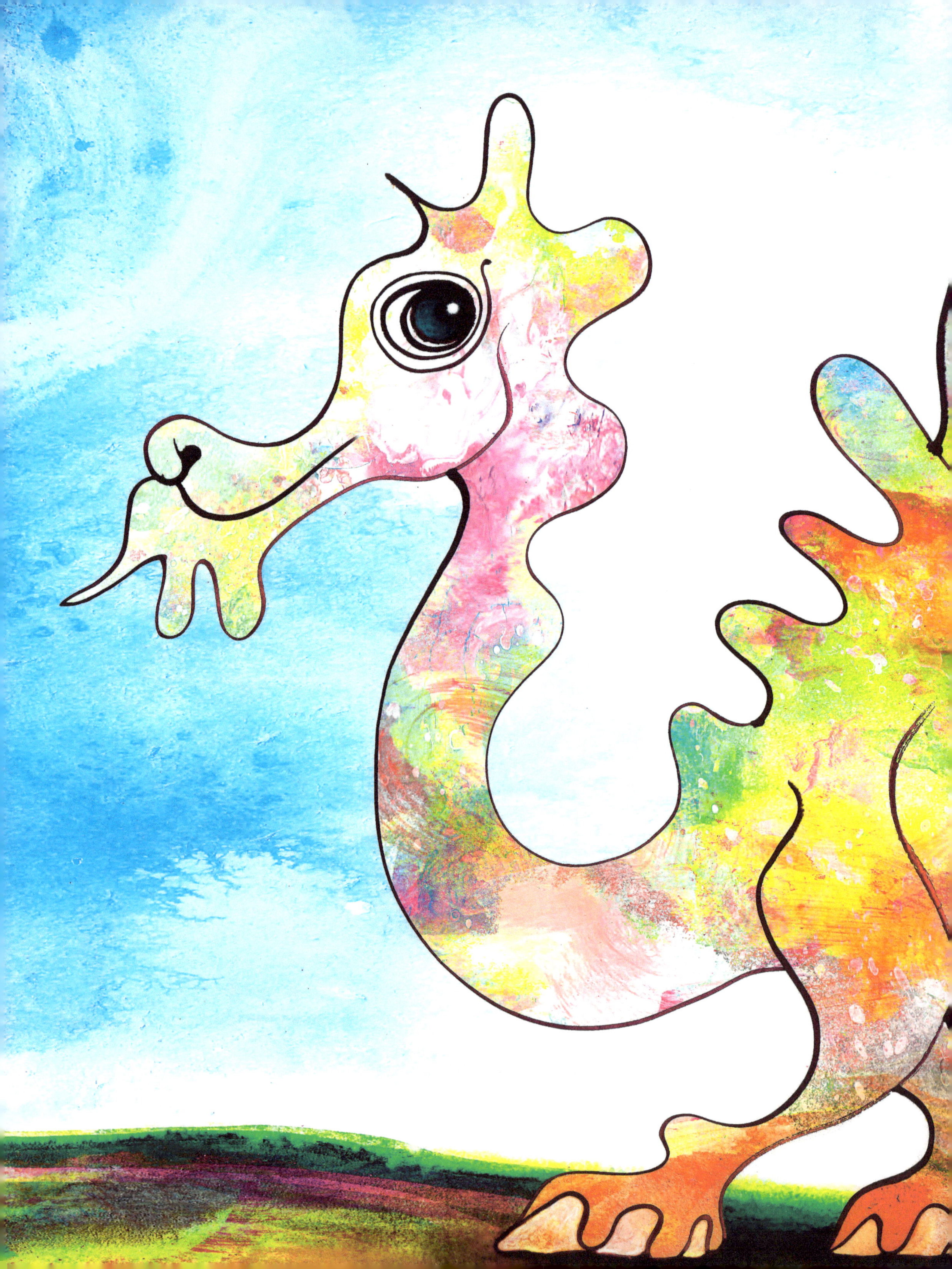

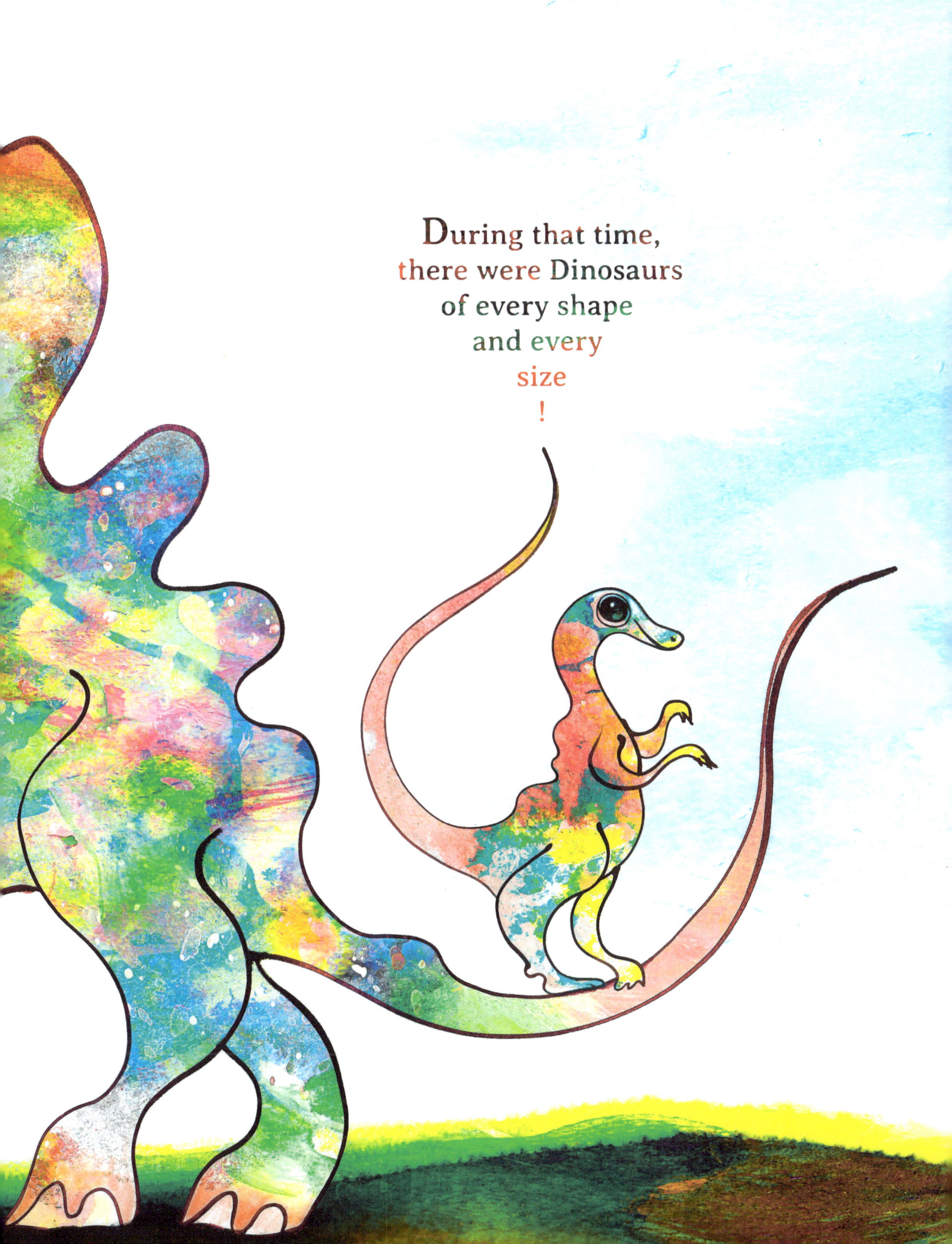

During that time,
there were Dinosaurs
of every shape
and every
size
!

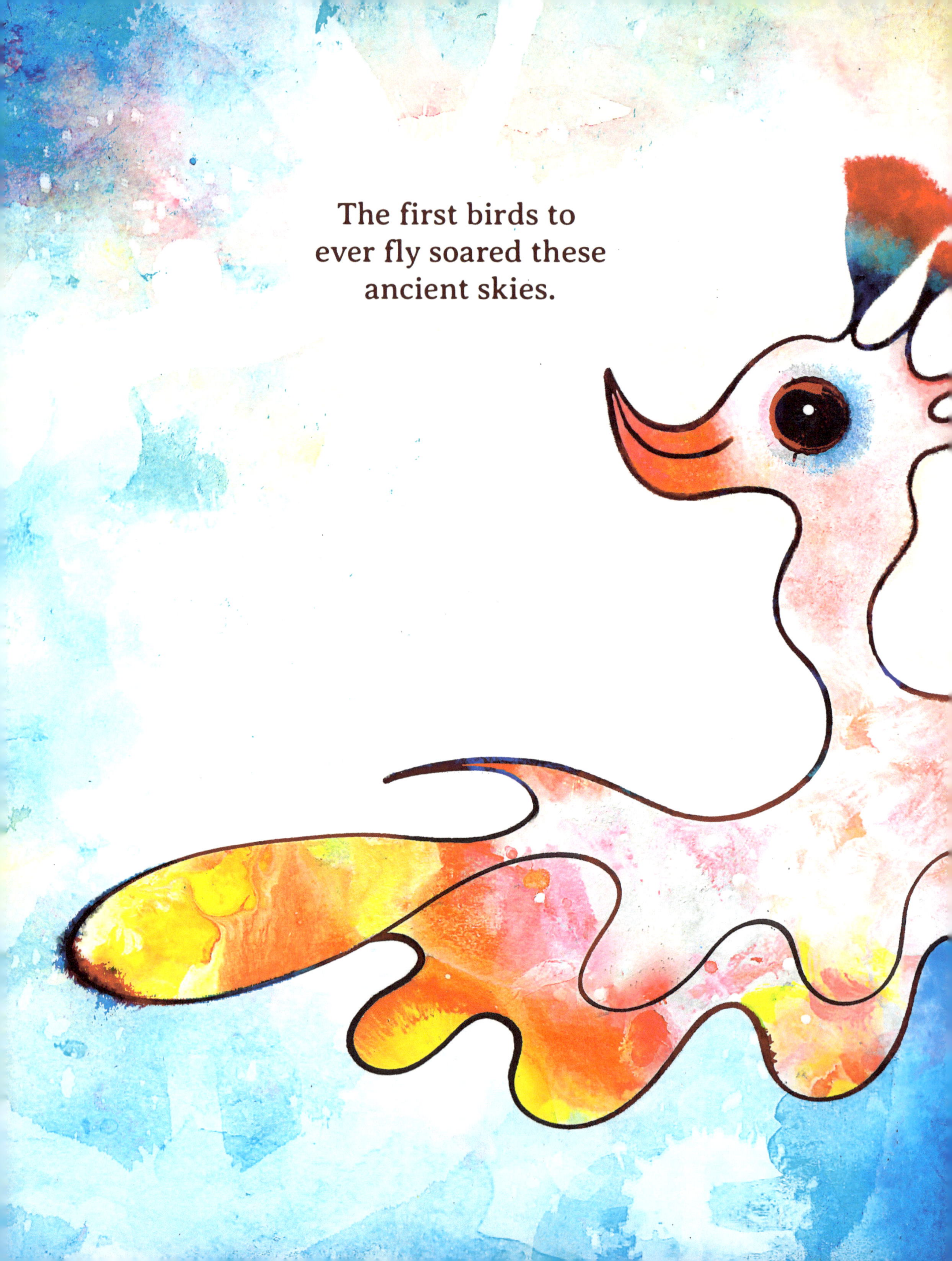
The first birds to
ever fly soared these
ancient skies.

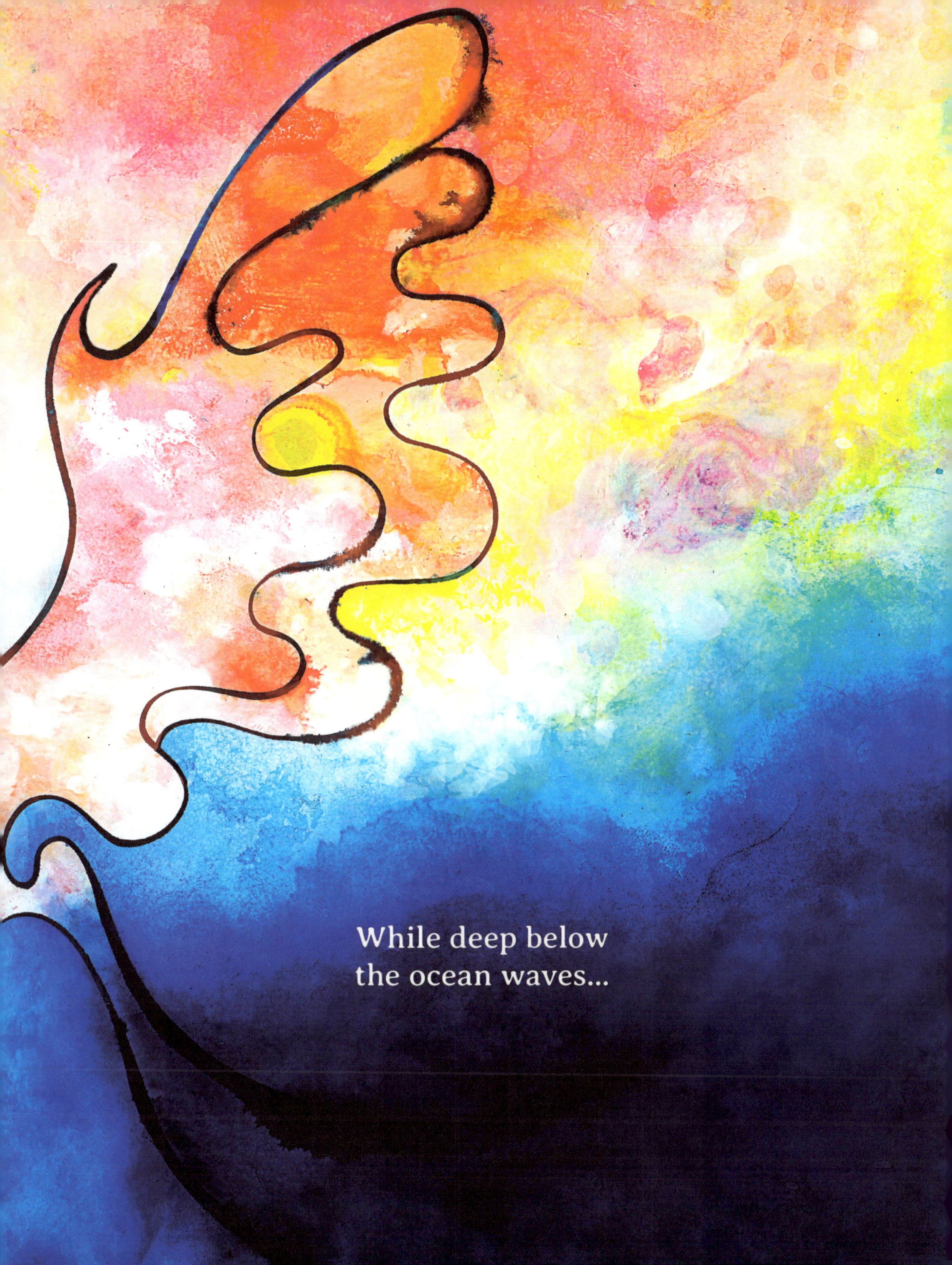

While deep below
the ocean waves...

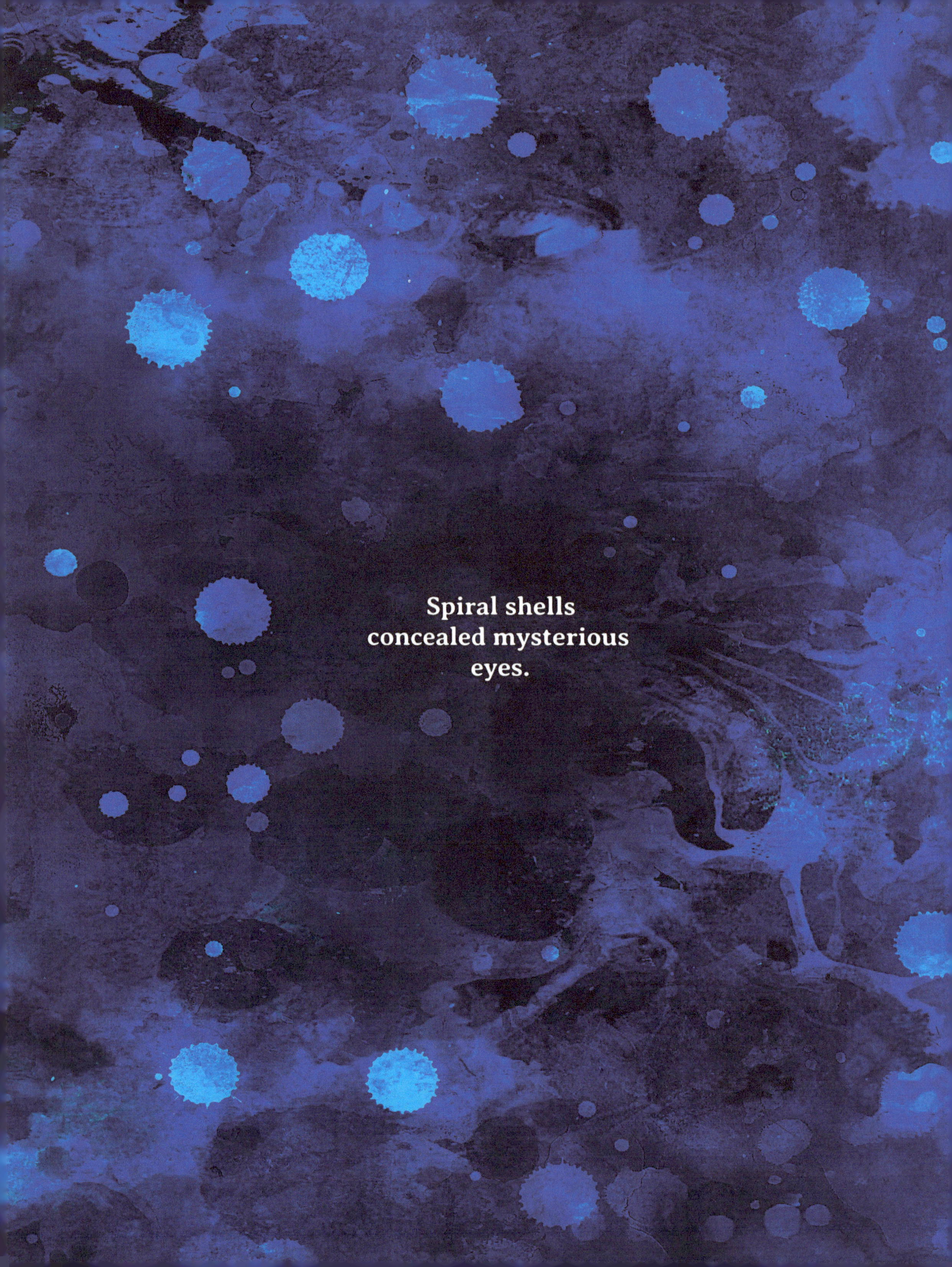
Spiral shells
concealed mysterious
eyes.

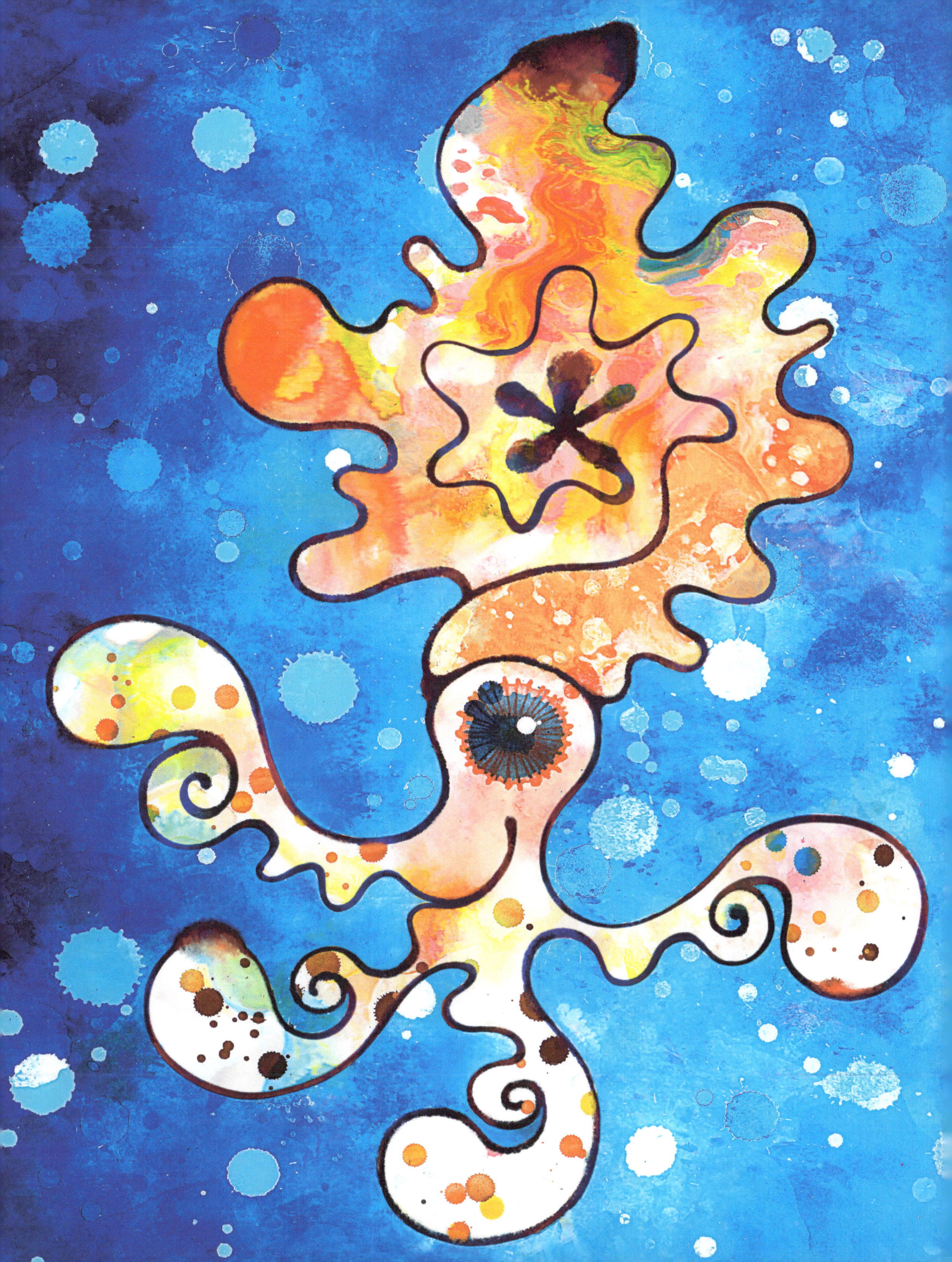

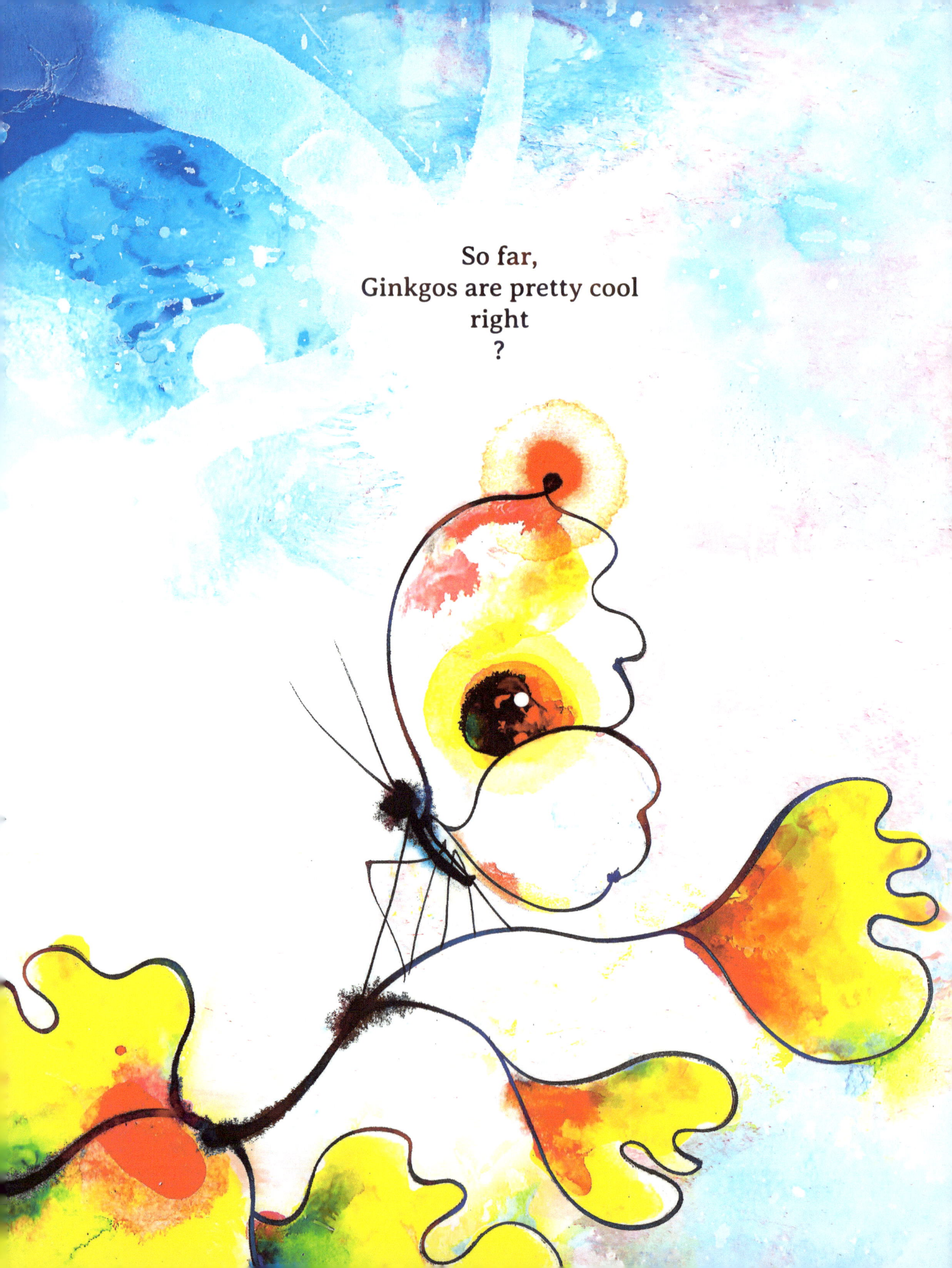

So far,
Ginkgos are pretty cool
right
?

There's something else
very special about them
and it is hidden from
sight.

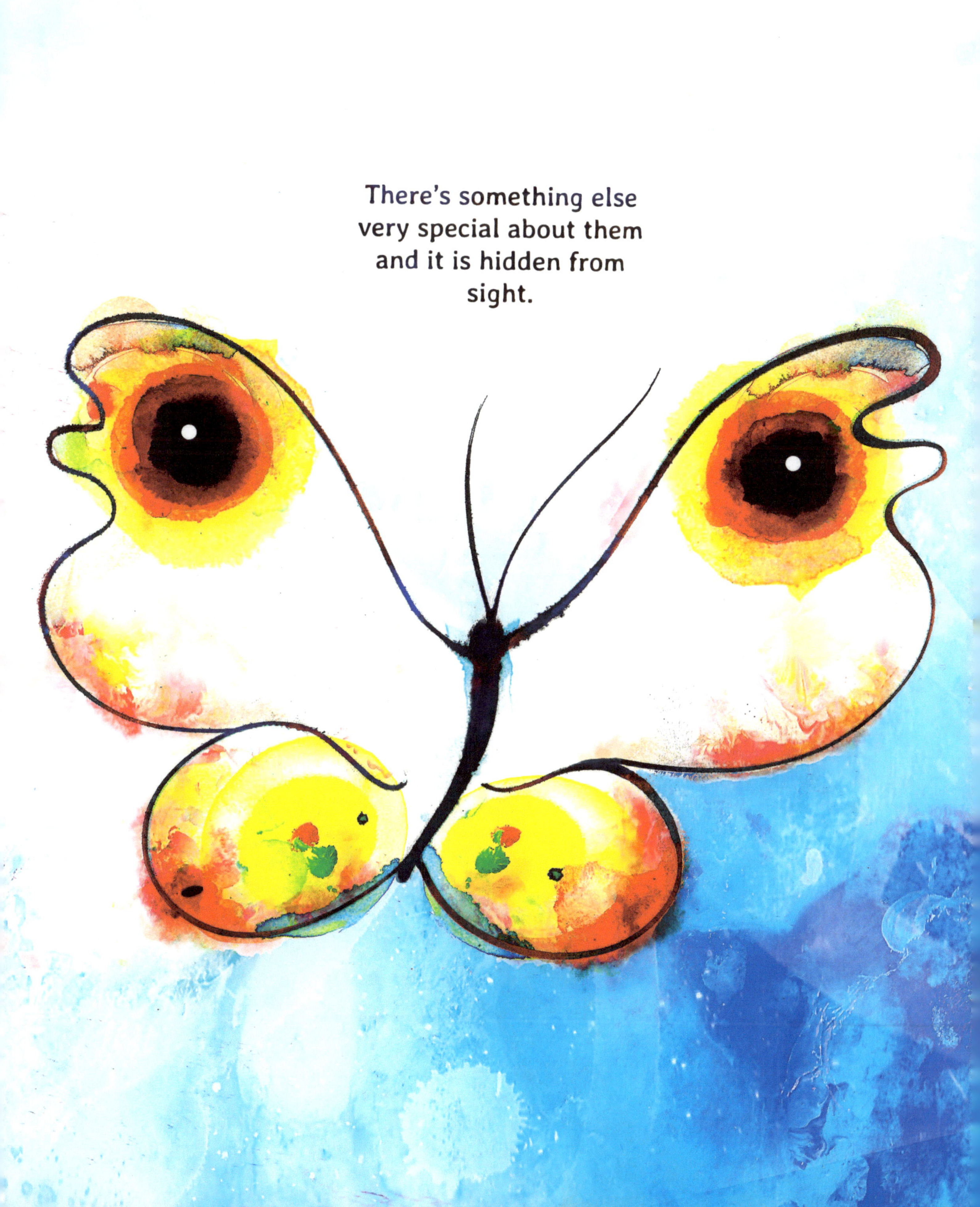

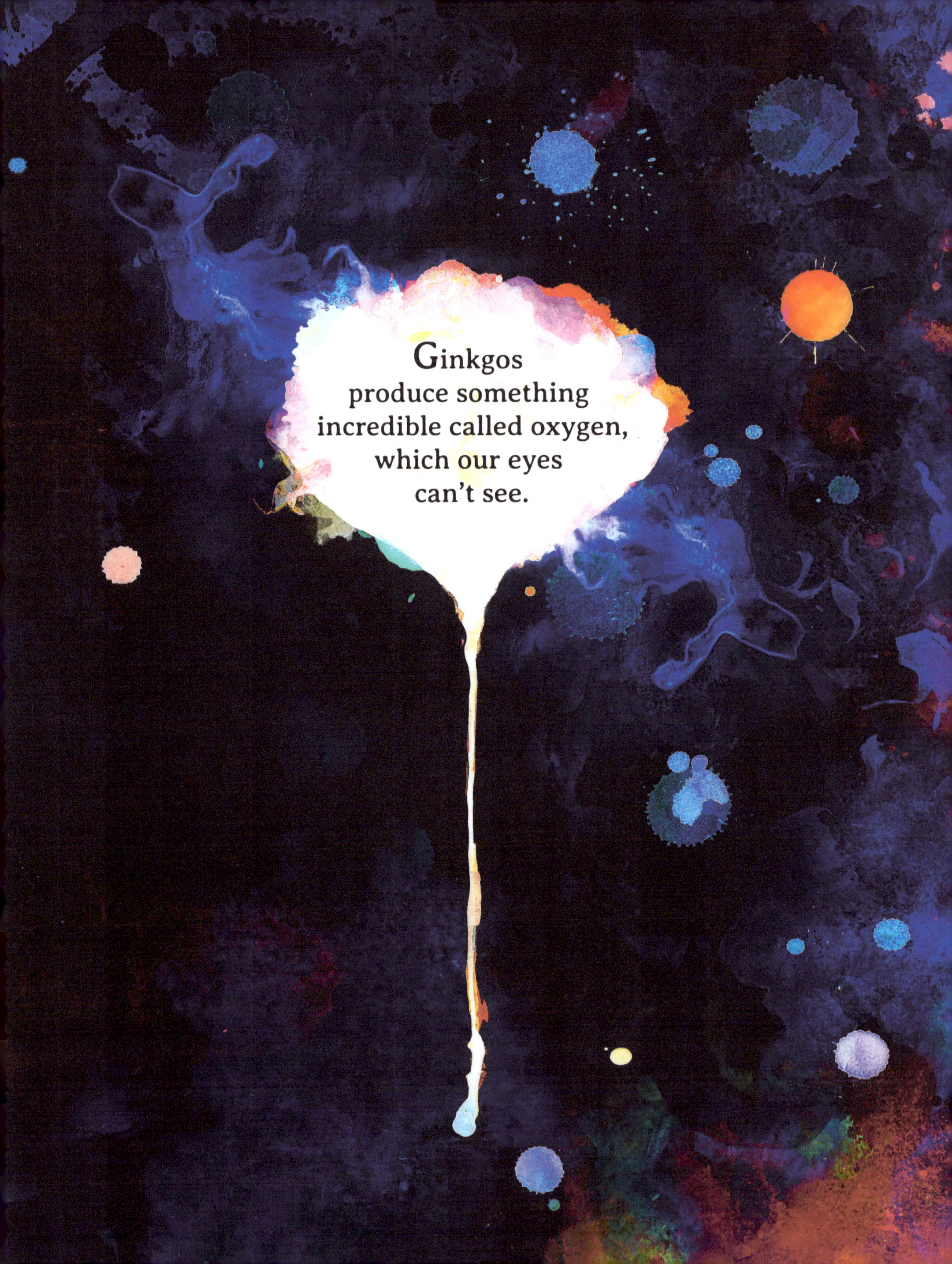

Ginkgos
produce something
incredible called oxygen,
which our eyes
can't see.

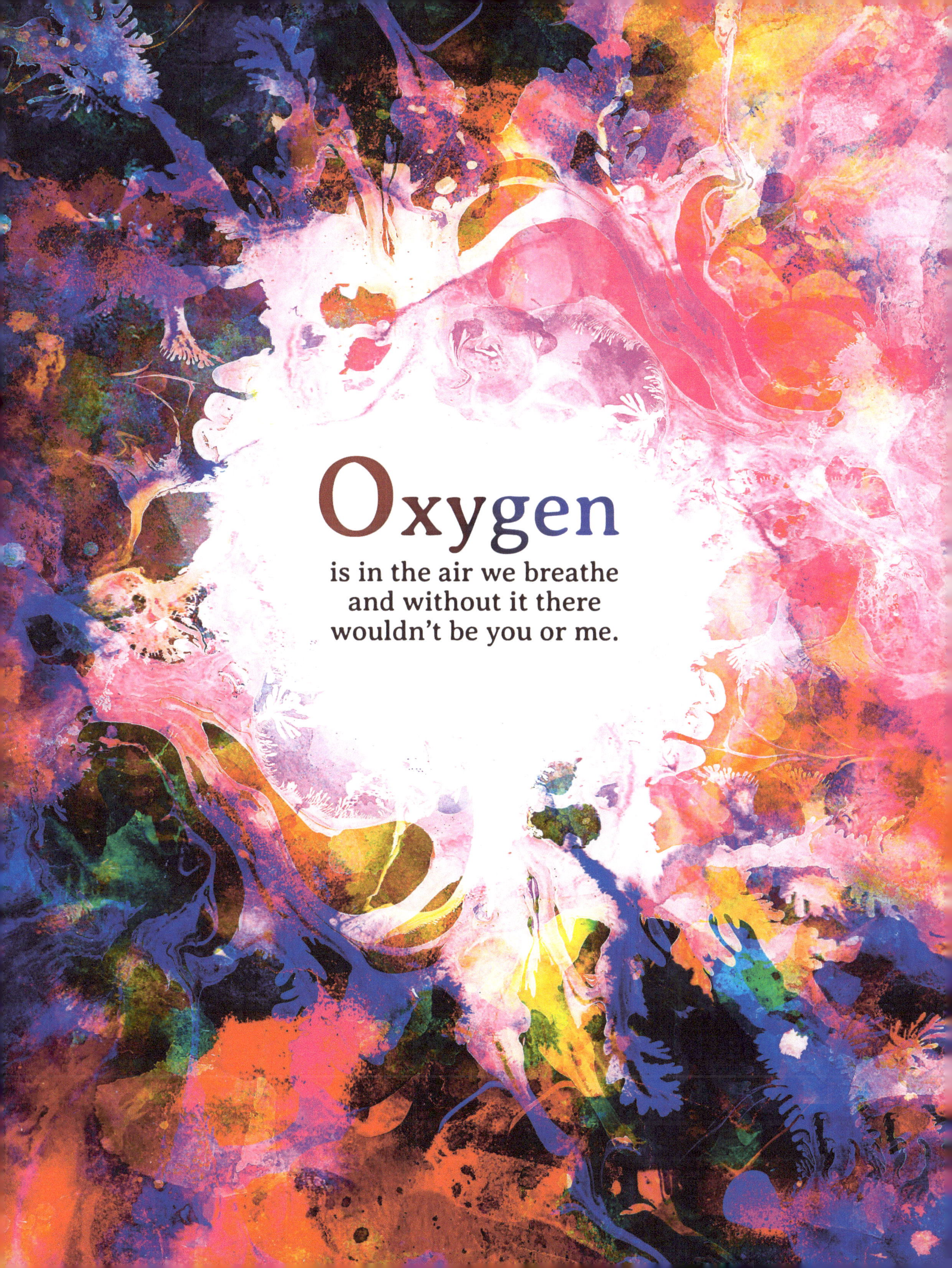
Oxygen
is in the air we breathe
and without it there
wouldn't be you or me.

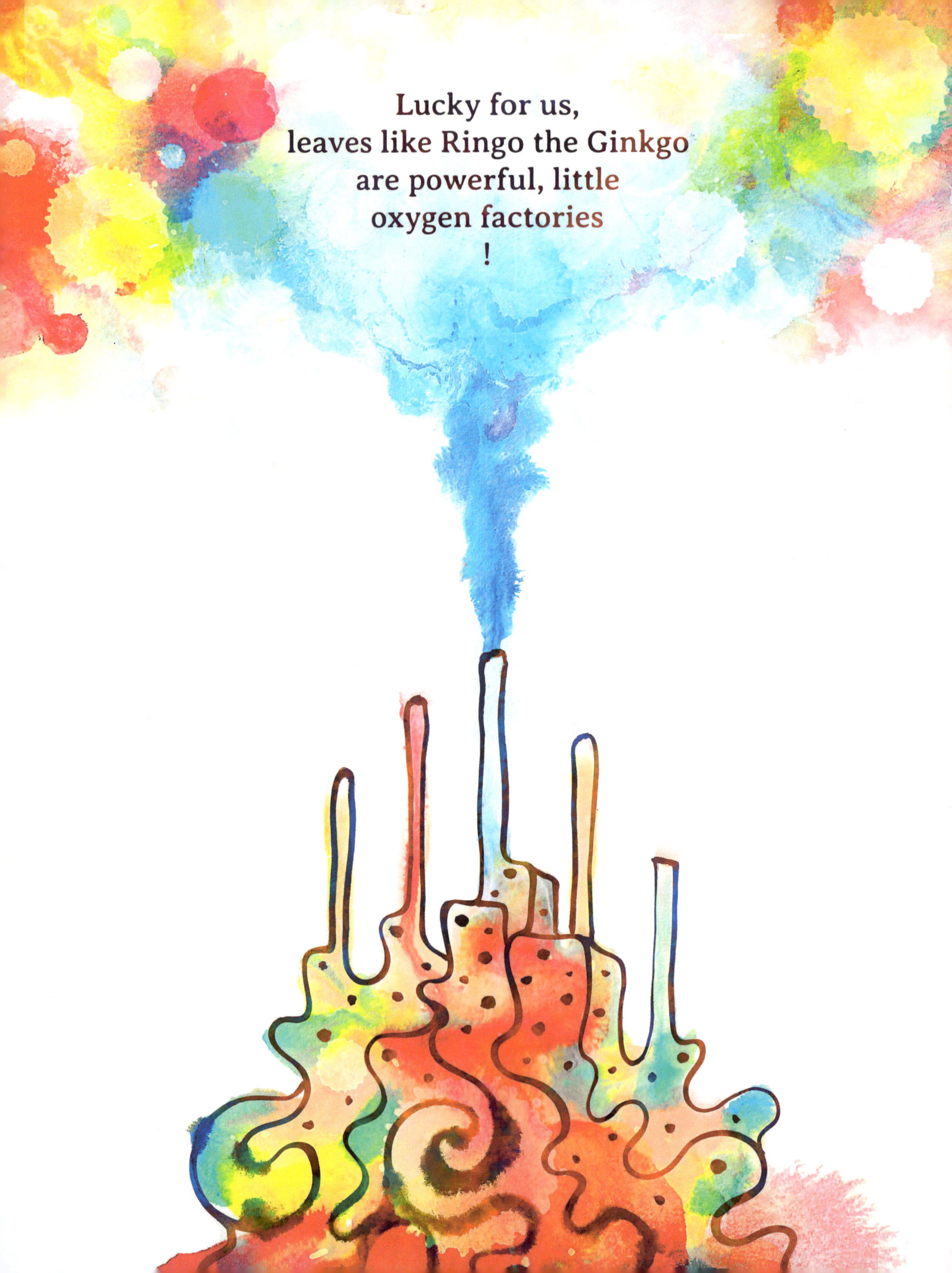

Lucky for us,
leaves like Ringo the Ginkgo
are powerful, little
oxygen factories
!

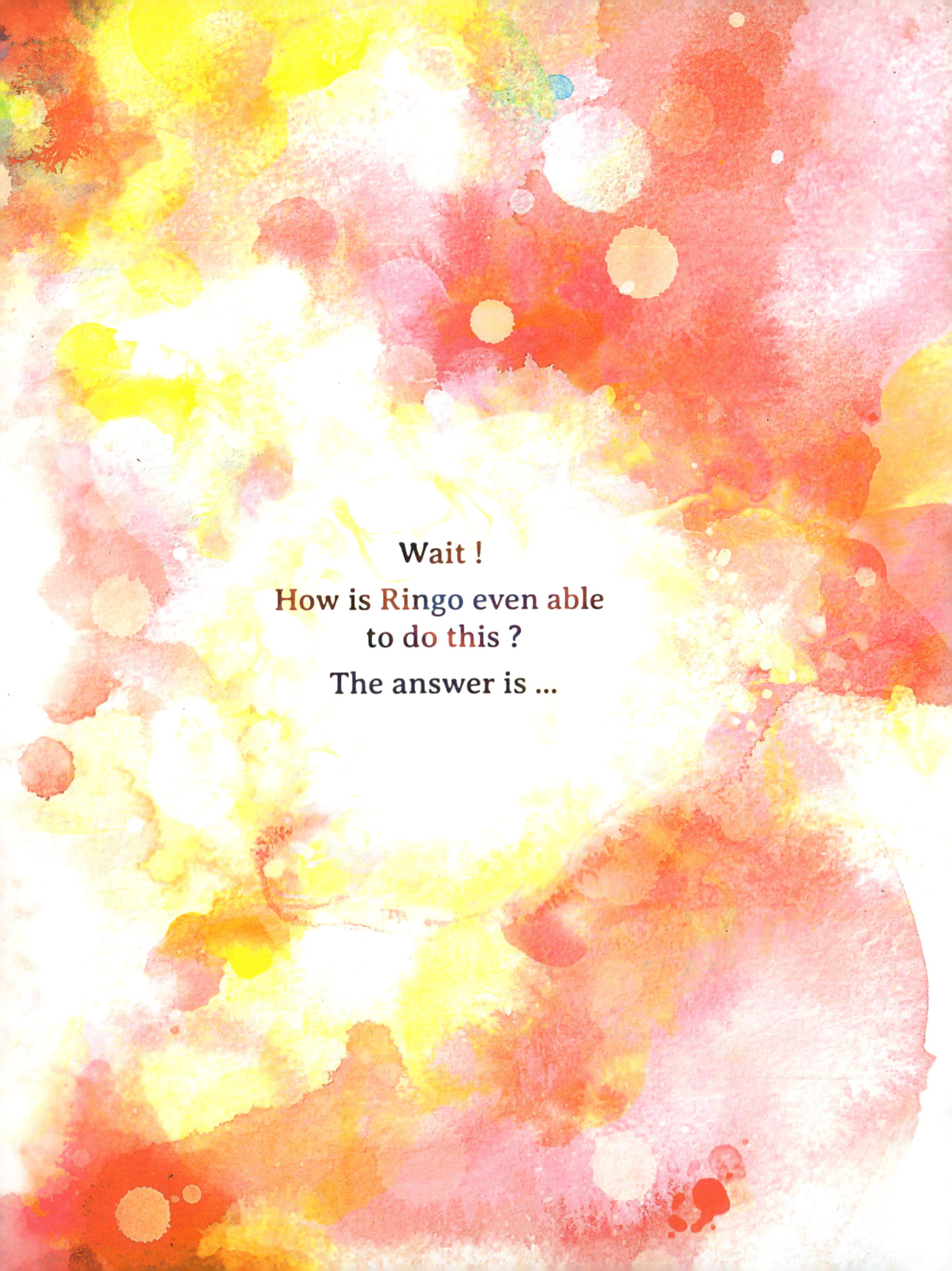
Wait !
How is Ringo even able
to do this ?
The answer is ...

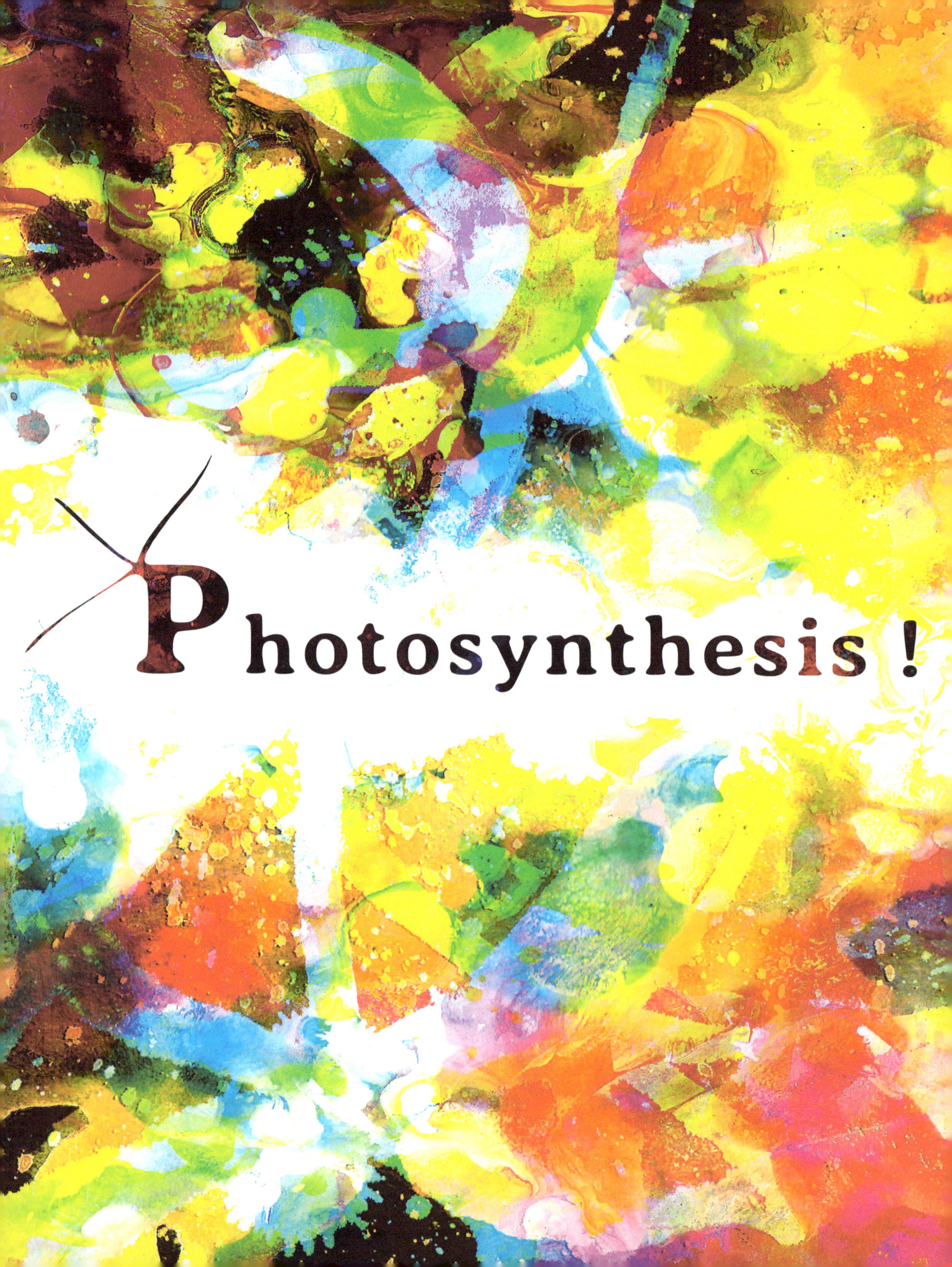
Photosynthesis !

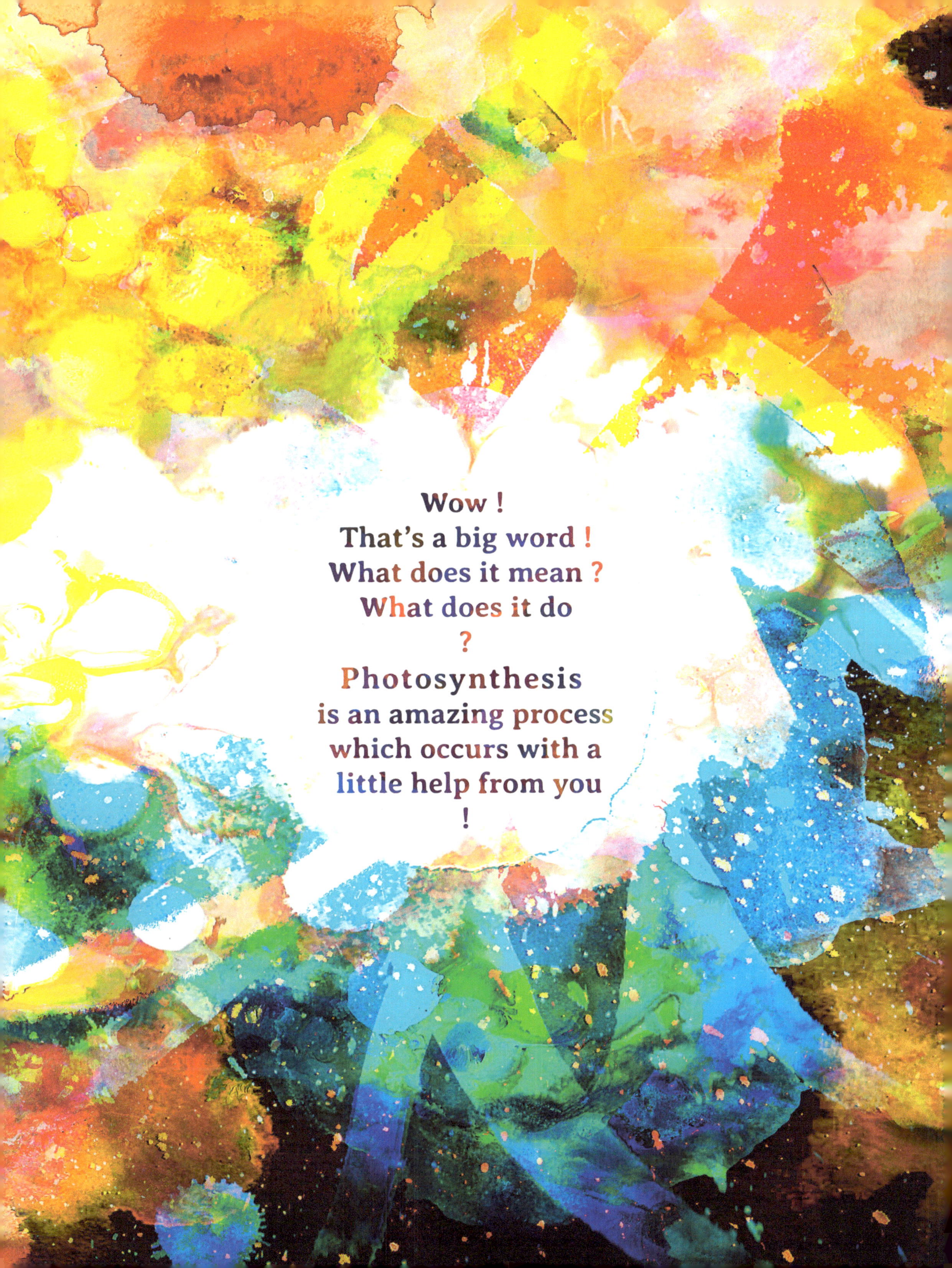

Wow !
That's a big word !
What does it mean ?
What does it do
?
Photosynthesis
is an amazing process
which occurs with a
little help from you
!

Take
a deep breath,
now let it
out.

You
just created
something that no
plant could live
without
!

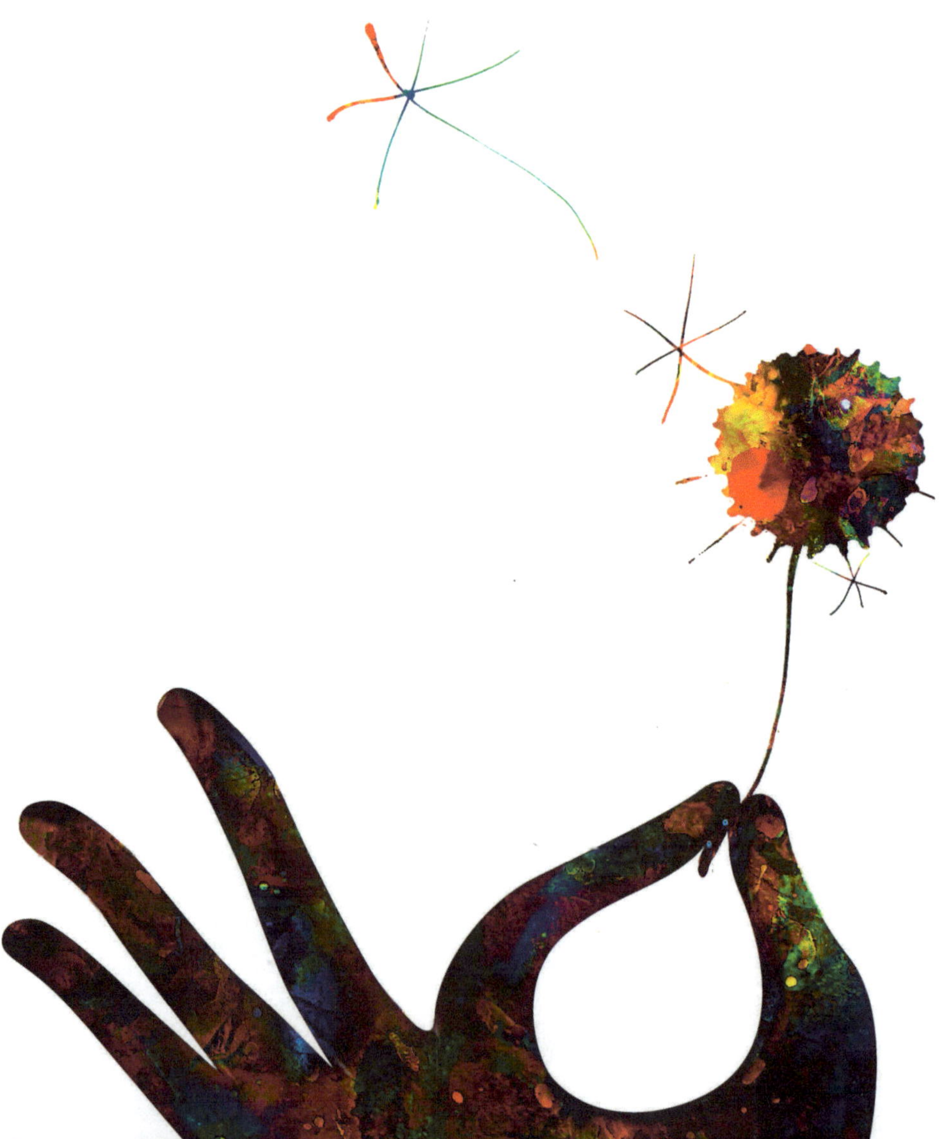

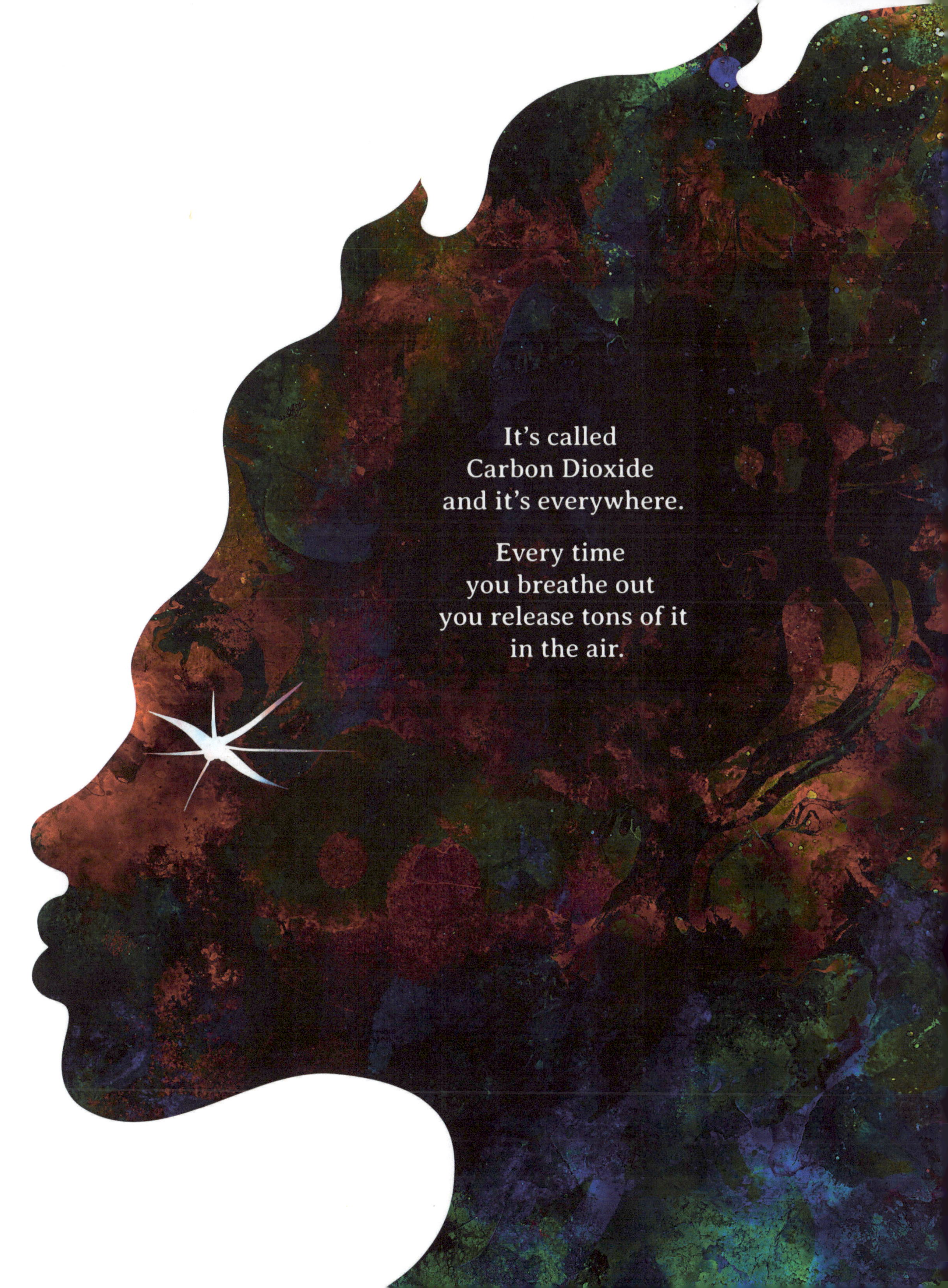

It's called
Carbon Dioxide
and it's everywhere.

Every time
you breathe out
you release tons of it
in the air.

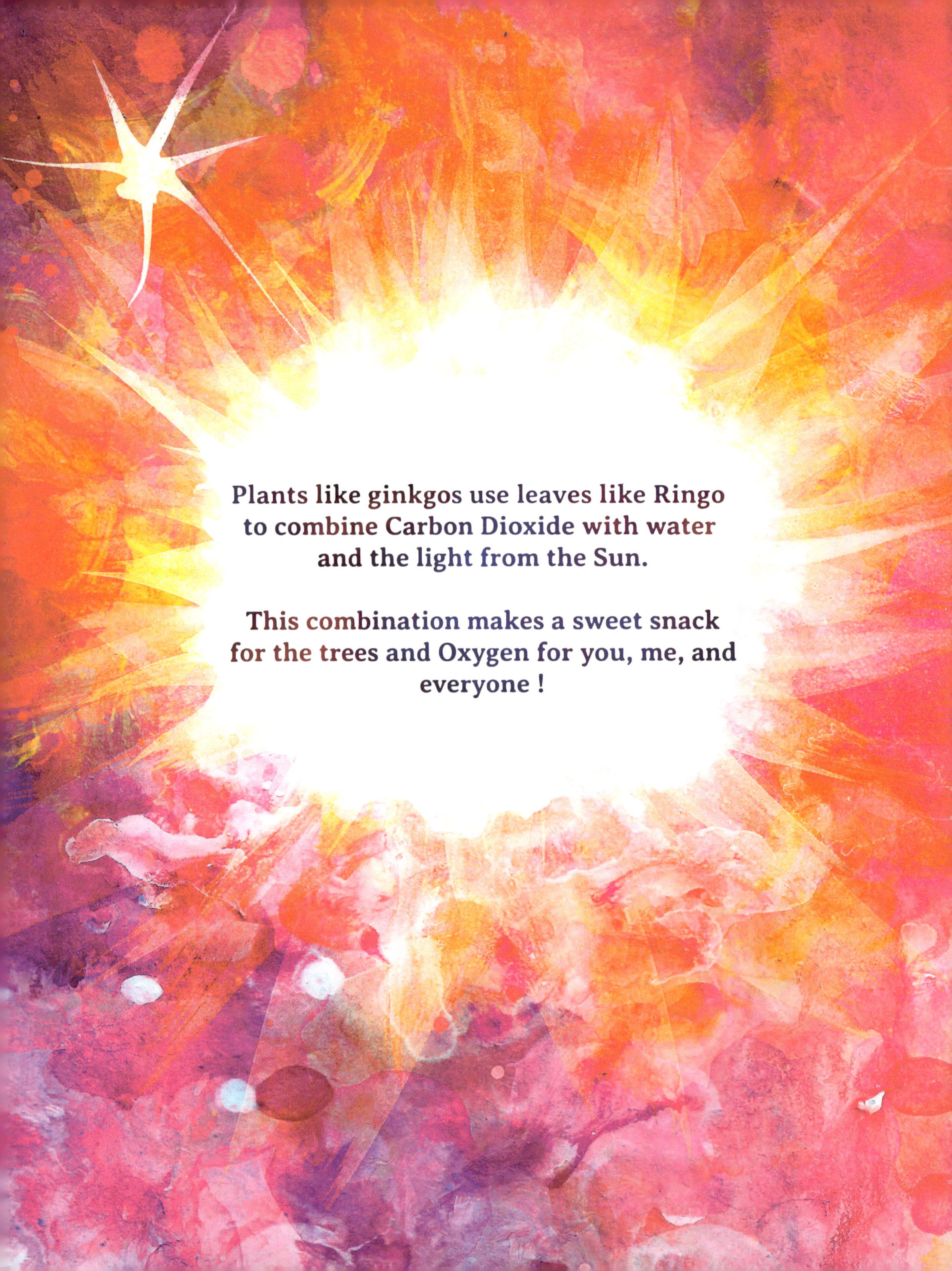
Plants like ginkgos use leaves like Ringo
to combine Carbon Dioxide with water
and the light from the Sun.

This combination makes a sweet snack
for the trees and Oxygen for you, me, and
everyone !

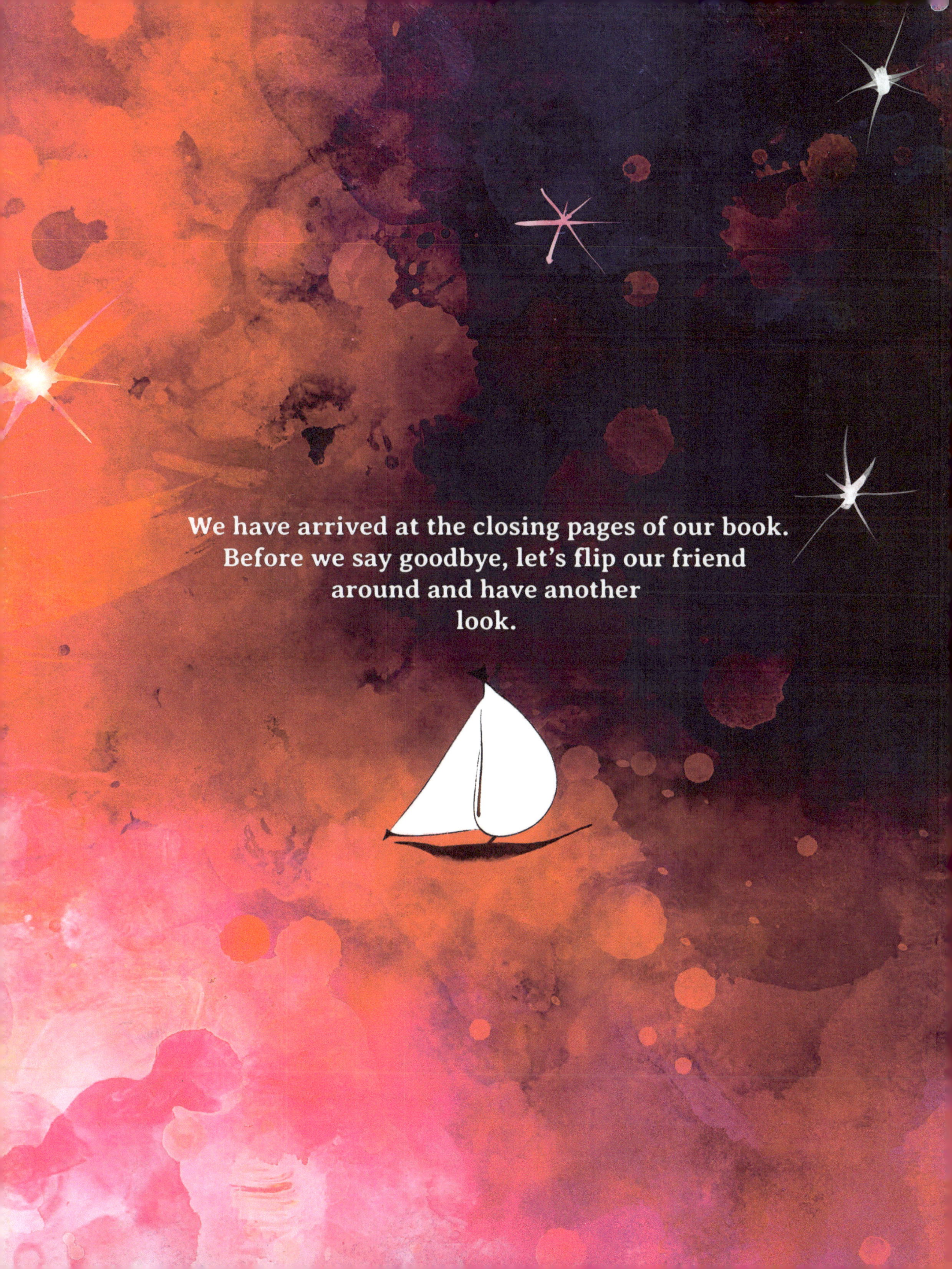
We have arrived at the closing pages of our book.
Before we say goodbye, let's flip our friend
around and have another
look.

Doesn't
Ringo now look like
a shiny, golden

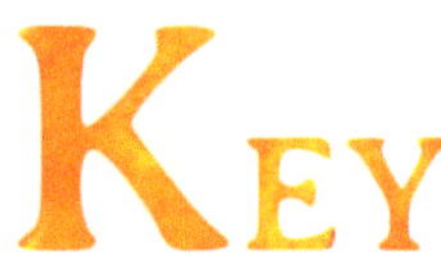

KEY

?

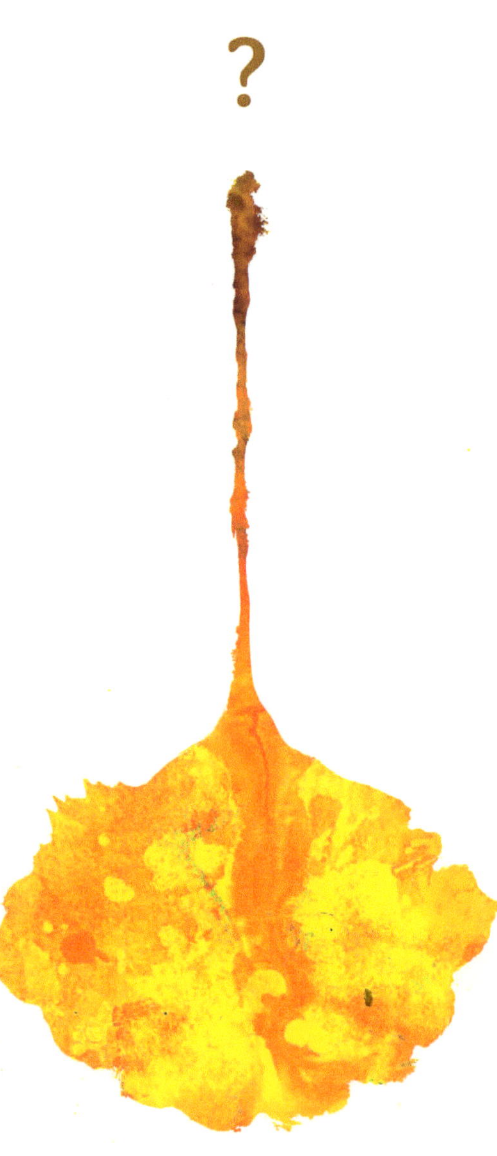

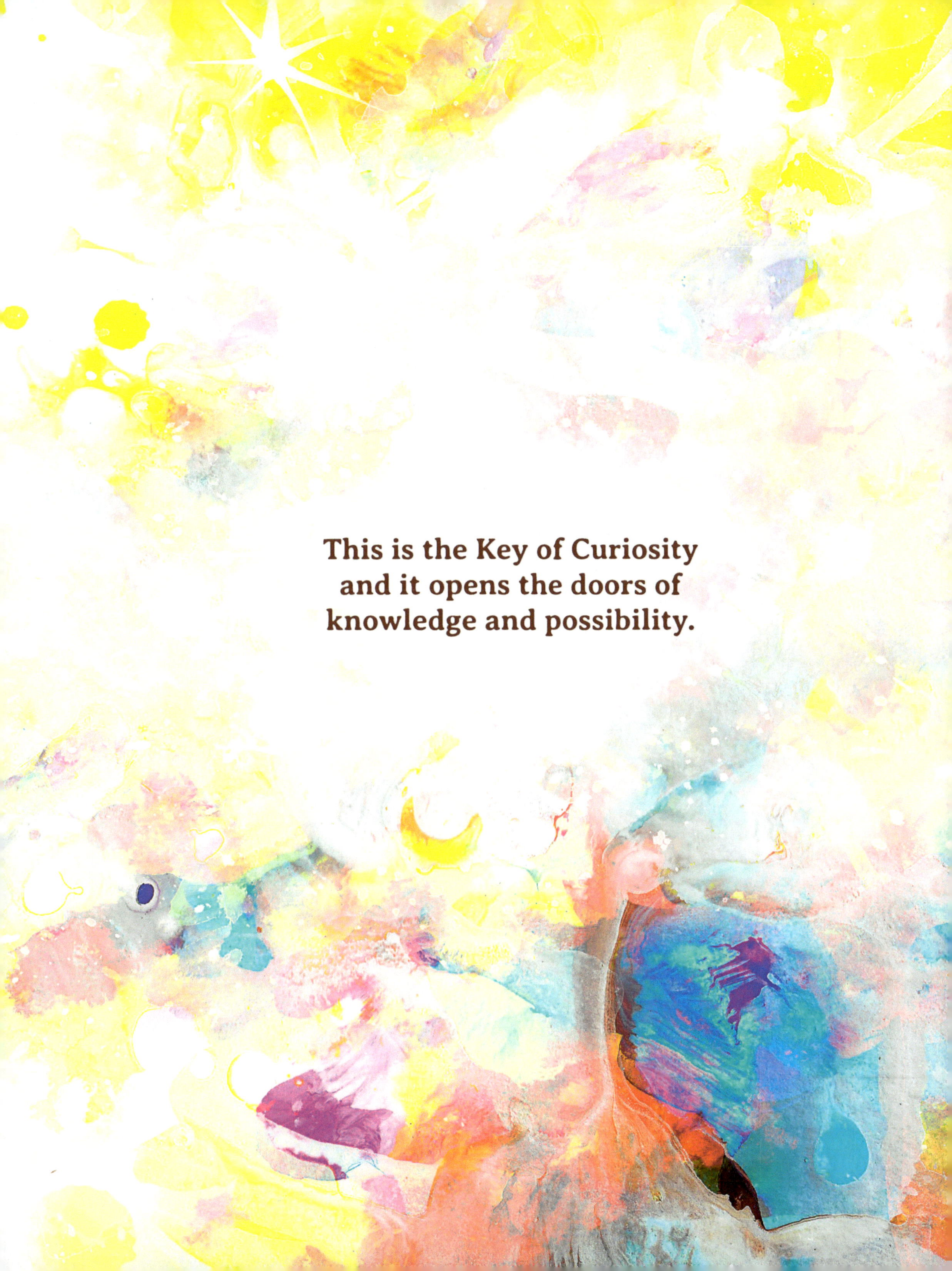

This is the Key of Curiosity
and it opens the doors of
knowledge and possibility.

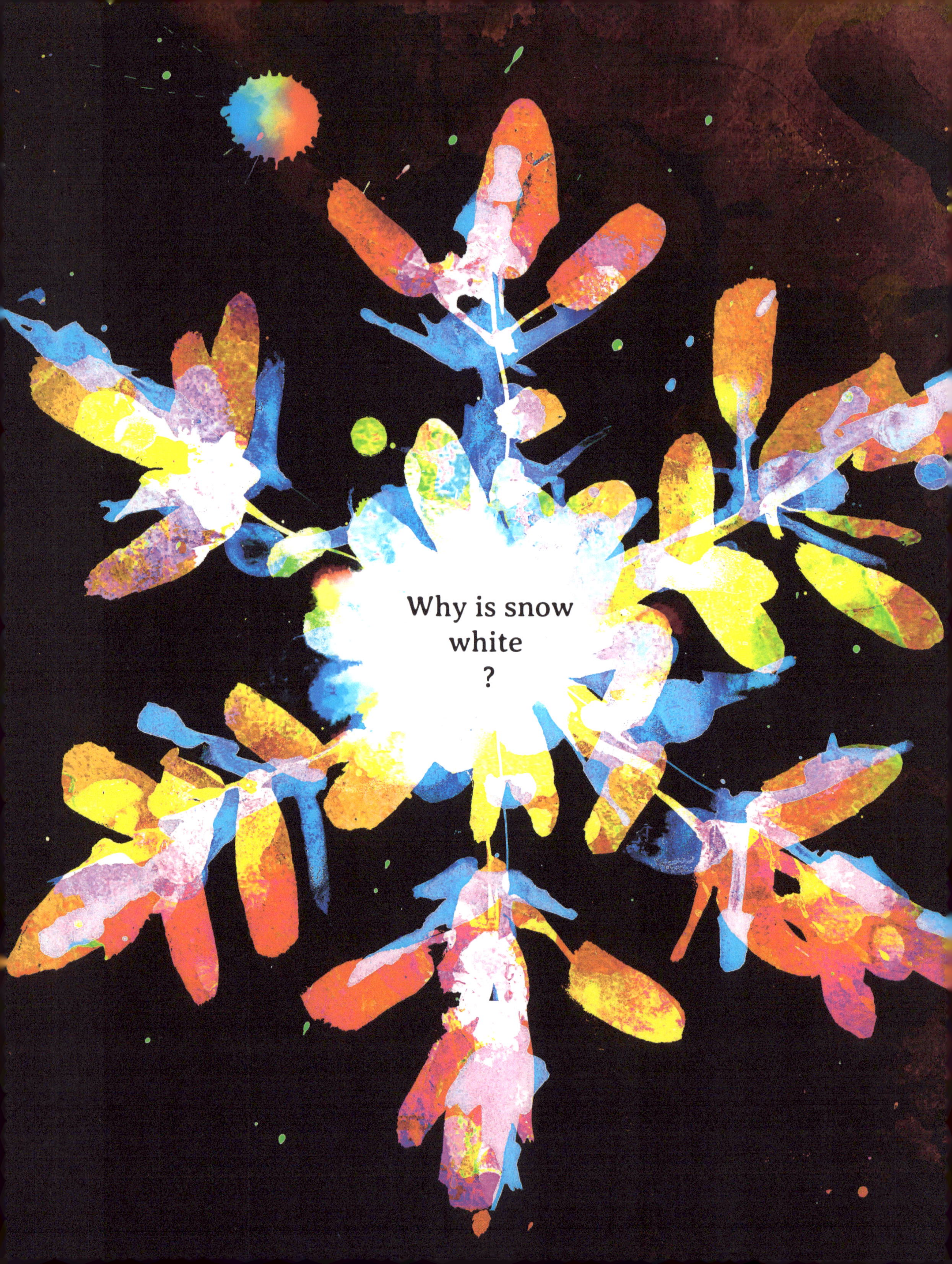
Why is snow
white
?

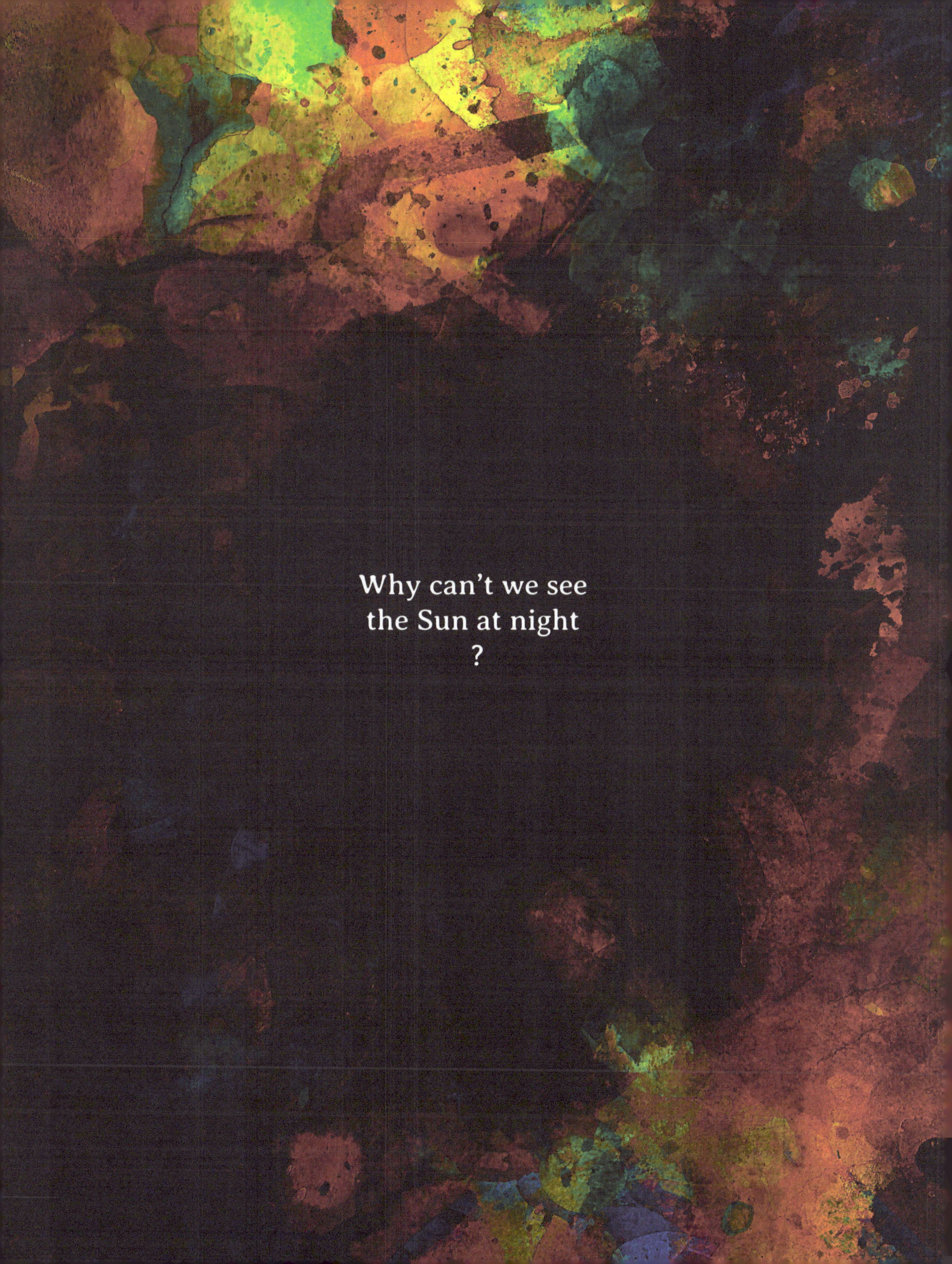
Why can't we see
the Sun at night
?

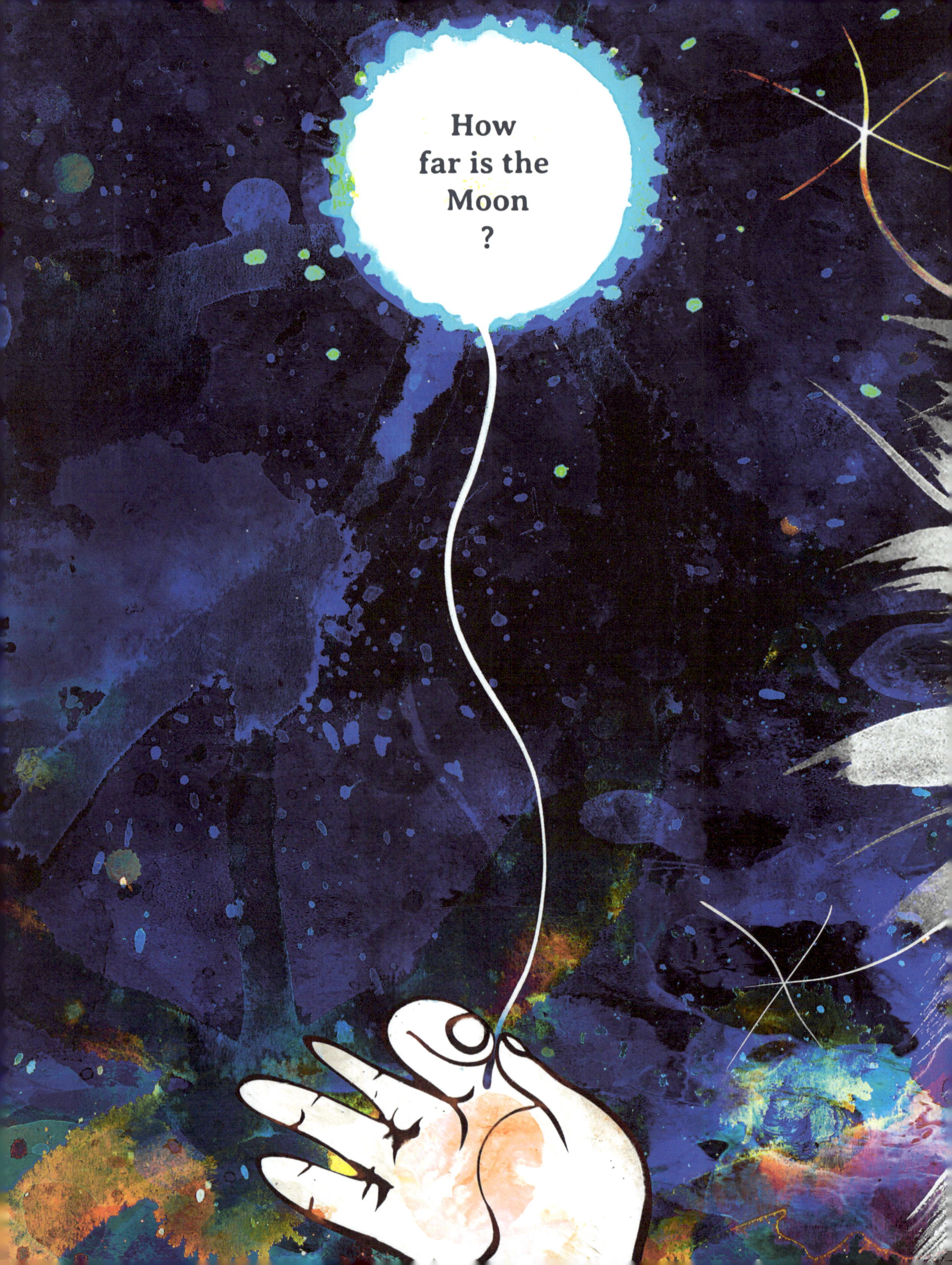

How
far is the
Moon
?

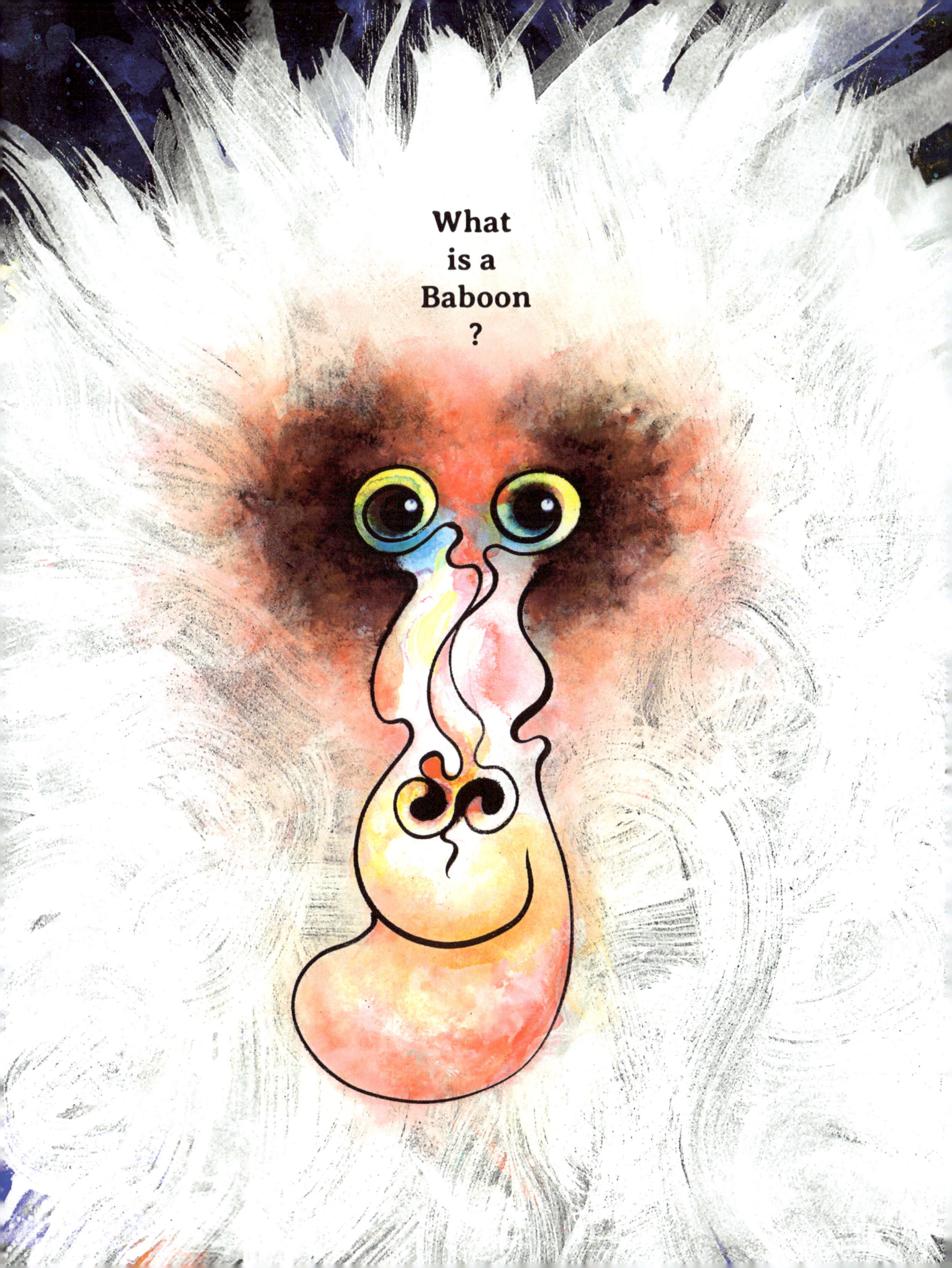
What
is a
Baboon
?

No one can answer these questions
better than you !

Just use your Key of Curiosity.
That's all you have to do.

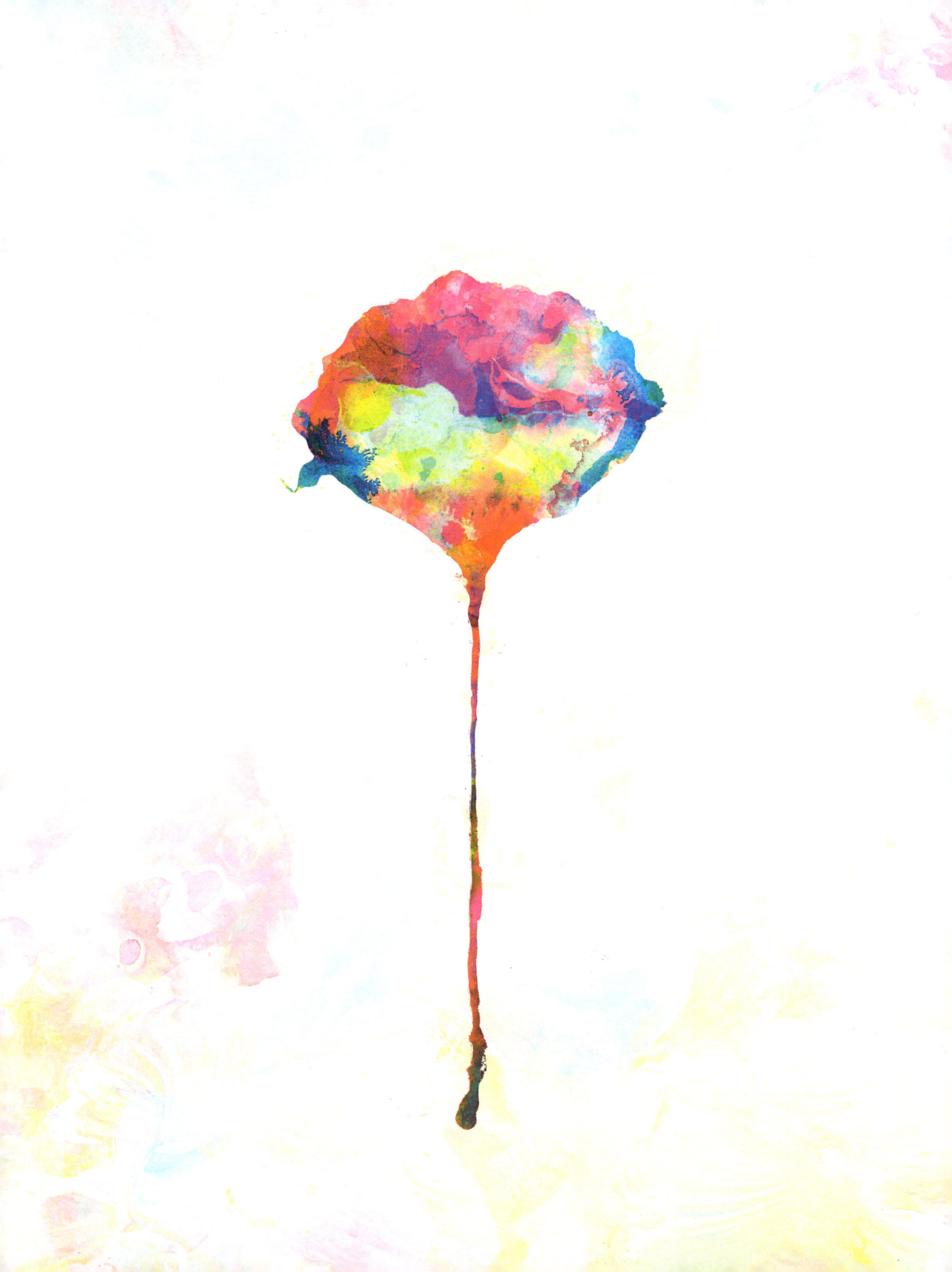